Managing
a Successful
Business
Turnaround

Managing
a Successful
Business
Turnaround

John Stewart Jr.

93 -753

amacom

AMERICAN MANAGEMENT ASSOCIATIONS

Library of Congress Cataloging in Publication Data

Stewart, John, Jr.
    Managing a successful business turnaround.

    Includes index.
    1. Organizational change.   2. Management.
3. Success in business.   I. Title
HD58.8.S73   1984   658.4'06   83-73037
ISBN 0-8144-5784-3
ISBN 0-8144-7608-2 (pbk.)

Printing number

10 9 8 7 6 5 4 3 2 1

*To my wife
and complete partner
Rachel*

Preface

MANAGING a rapid business turnaround is as easy as it is enjoyable and rewarding. Of course, it's enjoyable and rewarding. You've saved your company's life and brought peace of mind to your employees and their families, as well as to the owners, customers, vendors, and bankers. But easy? Yes! Easy!

A common element in the conversations I've had with other executives who have effected turnarounds is that the successful turnaround took less time and was not as difficult as they had anticipated.

This book sets forth a program that has been polished through four successful turnarounds of faltering businesses—businesses ranging from $10 million to $150 million in annual sales.

One turnaround involved a company that had had 13 consecutive years of diminishing returns, the last 7 tinged in red. In eight months the company was substantially in the black again.

Another involved a division that I took over not knowing that corporate management had already decided to liquidate it. That division became healthy and profitable in three months.

The third, involving a division with a long tradition of bouncing just above and below the break-even line, required almost a year to reach a satisfactory earnings level.

The fourth business was still profitable but com-

pletely demoralized after 18 months of drastically reduced earnings. There, the drain was plugged in 3
months. But due to extremely recessive economic conditions, it took another year to double both sales and
the rate of earnings.

The turnaround program described here contains
nothing dramatically new. A number of the principles
mentioned are taught in Management I at our colleges.
All the individual techniques discussed have been adequately covered in management texts and seminars. The
strength of this treatise lies in its simple, yet comprehensive, application of already-accepted management
practices to the singular task of turning a business
around.

The response of my management friends who first
received the proposed outline for this book was unani-
mous: "Too elementary. Kid stuff. There isn't one thing
in there that I didn't already know." What a kick in the
ego that was.

Thank goodness those same friends began calling
back with comments like this: "It finally dawned on me.
The outline is so simple, so basic, so far below the sophistication level of enlightened management that I
didn't give it my full attention at first. But for some reason it haunted me. Then I realized that for the same
reason that I had glossed over your outline, I had also
neglected some of those basic techniques in running my
business. Thanks for getting me back on track."

One friend, who operates a small scrap yard, further
fortified my decision to proceed with this manuscript
when he reported immediate profit-producing results
after implementing a few of the recommended techniques. This book, while directed primarily at manufacturing concerns, can be applied to most types of businesses.

One word of caution. This book is in a similar category with most good consultants and most good staff
personnel. It can help in turning a business around, and

it can help in reversing the poor performance of a single department. *It can help.* But *it cannot make it happen.*

A successful business turnaround can be executed only by honest, intelligent line management. If you want your business turned around, *you* are going to have to do it. You will be able to enlist all the capable, enthusiastic help you need. You will be able to delegate many elements of the program to others. But the job will not get done without a total commitment from you, the top line manager. The resulting enjoyment and satisfaction will be ample reward for that degree of dedication.

Another requirement for a successful business turnaround is common sense. This principle comes into play at the very beginning of the process, when you consider that a turnaround is actually a journey that the company is about to embark on.

Therefore, the same simple four questions used in planning a personal vacation are applicable here:

1. *Where am I starting from?* Make a comprehensive and accurate assessment of what and where the company is now in terms of market, products/ services, and financial, physical, and human resources.
2. *Where do I want to go?* Select longer-range objectives in terms of markets served, growth, and financial returns.
3. *How do I want to get there?* Choose the strategies, or routes, that will lead the company to its established objectives.
4. *What mileposts will I pass along the way? When will I arrive at each one? What will my financial condition be at each one?* You and your staff will need to draw up a series of control reports, denoting interim goals, measuring progress to those goals, and designed to keep the program on course.

These four questions will surface throughout this book, as they should throughout your turnaround program. How well you answer them, especially in regard to strategic long-range planning (Chapter 13), will have considerable impact on the results of your turnaround.

In addition to strong line management leadership, and to considering a turnaround as you would plan a trip, there are four other basic ingredients to a successful turnaround. They, too, are so obvious that many managers tend to slip on the banana peel of assumption that they already exist, by definition, in the enterprise. The fact is that organizations that do possess these four ingredients seldom need a turnaround. These ingredients are:

1. A commitment to change on the part of the top line manager. Certainly a company that needs a turnaround to catch up with competition has been doing something wrong. Something must be changed.

From my experience, lack of commitment to change is the major cause for failure in privately held companies. Time and again I have seen such firms pay hefty fees for sound consultant advice and then disregard that advice completely. In essence, the top manager says: "I want my company turned around. But I don't want anyone to change the way we do things here. No big waves. My people have been with me for years. They are 110 percent loyal to me. I don't want to upset them."

In a sense, I admire such entrepreneurs. Yet, if they only knew how much happier the vast majority of their people would be in a profitable, dynamic environment ... if they could only recognize the long-range negative consequences of such an attitude!

Family firms, however, do not hold exclusive rights to such a position. Once, upon accepting a turnaround assignment for a very large publicly held corporation, I was handed a list of "untouchables." The list included the names of about a dozen managers who were to be exempted from any change in their employment status during the turnaround program. As you might suspect, the people on that list had been key contributors to the firm's need for a turnaround. Untouchability had be-

come synonymous with unaccountability, which had
provided significant quantities of red ink. The "untouchables" retained their status. But, as a result, that
particular turnaround took twice as long.

2. *Sound, organized assessment of problems and opportunities.* Shaky businesses seem to be blessed with a
plethora of excellent programs that, instead of improving their position, end up tightening the financial
chokehold. These great ideas make a fortune for other
companies. Why don't they work for every business that's
in trouble? Usually, it is because they fail to address the
most pressing needs of the company or they do so in a
disorganized manner.

I am vividly reminded of a firm I had joined at the
time of its annual planning meeting. This firm was in
financial trouble, but no one would ever have guessed it
from the glowing forecasts made at the planning sessions.

I had an opportunity to study the presentations during meeting breaks and after adjournment of the daily
sessions. I found that: (1) the forecasts were considerably better in the areas of sales income and expense reduction than had ever been accomplished, (2) they included no valid, specific plans to achieve such
improvements, and (3) the individual departmental
projections appeared to have come from separate, au-
tonomous companies. None of the figures matched.

The participants fell into disgruntled shock when I
announced my findings at the celebration dinner. That
shock intensified after I showed them that the company
could not break even in the coming year, even at the
level of their inflated sales forecast. The assessment on
which that plan had been based was neither sound nor
organized.

During the all-night regrouping workshop that followed, a staff member advanced a brilliant solution: The
company served five distinct markets with similar
products. These products, listed in five separate catalogs did, however, differ slightly. It was suggested that

if customers were permitted to mix and match accoutrements from each of the five catalogs, sales could be increased by 50 percent over the preceeding year. My check of this theory supported its viability. The recommended change was made policy. And the meeting adjourned as a delayed success.

The disaster was not long in arriving. Manufacturing could not come close to profitable production at catalog prices when forced into the resulting infinite number of product permutations. The second assessment had been organized—but far from sound.

3. Capable, committed people working together and enjoying it. I said earlier that turnarounds are usually easy to achieve. There is, however, one difficult step: In almost every case, a few people will be hurt.

People are the keys to the success or failure of most companies. A firm in need of a turnaround almost surely needs to replace some key people. Fortunately, only a few people will be directly involved. Unfortunately, some loyal, respected employees will probably be in that few.

"Good old Joe. He's been here for twenty-five years. He's our most valuable manager. This place couldn't run without him. There are so many things we don't have on paper, and Joe has every one of them in his head. You can count on him to do anything you ask. All of our older employees think the world of Joe."

Hopefully, Joe will emerge as an untapped resource and contribute much to the turnaround program. But it may be that Joe has been faithfully operating the largest backhoe in digging the company rut. Every firm in need of a turnaround has some fine Joes and Marys who, through no fault of their own, are either hopelessly mired in the company rut or are beyond being rescued from over the peak of the Peter Principle.

It is important to comprehend this point and to quickly identify the Joes and Marys. It is just as important to make a special effort to retain them, channeling their knowledge into productive use. This helps preserve a sense of security in all levels of personnel, which may be of great value to the turnaround program.

However, as noted, retention of all key personnel is seldom advisable. And no matter how carefully you manage the removal of dedicated personnel, old-timers or recent additions, organizational trauma is the immediate result. That initial shock, though, soon changes into enthusiastic support, as performance begins to improve in what had been the problem areas and as people get caught up in the thrill of a turnaround.

Anyone who will be in the mainstream of the turnaround program and who is either not totally committed or fails to work closely with others toward common goals should be removed without compunction.

4. Creative, carefully planned, well-executed, and adequately controlled actions. Creativity is necessary to business success. But business turnarounds don't fail for the lack of in-house creativity. The secret is to sort out and harness the creativity that you have, so that through careful planning, good execution, and adequate controls, it produces profit.

I am reminded of a company whose R&D department was recognized as the best in its industry and frequently won acclaim for its design efforts. Unfortunately, that company was not in business merely to design products . . . but to produce and sell them as well. The company's Sales/Marketing group was extremely weak, and it had a very small market share. As a result, competitors with major market shares and/or strong Sales organizations were copying and selling most of the designs. To add insult to injury, there was no coordination between R&D, Engineering, and Manufacturing, with the consequence that most new products could not be produced for less than 30 percent above the intended cost. Poor planning, poor execution, no control.

Many managers could produce a successful business turnaround solely by concentrating on these four requirements and by utilizing specific techniques with which they are already familiar. This book is for those other managers, who would prefer a more detailed set of guidelines.

If you are in the second group, let's get on with it. There is a business to be turned around.

The chapters of this book are arranged in chronological order, each one describing a step in the turnaround process. A number of the steps can, however, be effected almost simultaneously.

I wish to thank my friend Alvin Jacobson for the suggestions and encouragement he contributed to this book.

John Stewart Jr.

Contents

1

Introduce the Program
to Key Members
of Your Staff

YOU are personally committed to leading a business turnaround. *You* have a good idea of the steps *you* plan to take. *You* are confident that *you* can do the job.

Now is the time to bring your immediate subordinates, your key personnel, into the action. They are to play important roles in the program and will be critical to its success. The sooner your key people are included, the sooner they will feel a part of the program and the more apt they will be to contribute enthusiastically to its success. At the same time, by bringing them in early in the game, you will have a head start in being able to evaluate their individual performances in the new environment of a turnaround. More on this point later.

Who should be included in this group? Generally, this group should consist of all and only those who report directly to you, the executive in charge of the turnaround. In some cases, depending on organizational considerations, a few more subordinates might be added in order to gain broader functional coverage.

The Kickoff Meeting

Call a noninterruptible, formal meeting of your turnaround staff. Be prepared with a three-section agenda:

an introduction, a program outline, and a few new ground rules. The meeting should take less than 90 minutes, and it must be carefully planned and conducted, so that it achieves the strong, positive impact required. Your staff must leave the meeting with the conviction that a turnaround can and will be made, beginning at once.

Introduction

This part of the agenda will vary, depending primarily on whether or not you are new to your position. In any case, the key feelings that you must instill in your staff during the introduction are confidence and optimism. Your staff members must be moved to believe that the company can be turned around rapidly and that you are the person who can do it.

This segment should be relatively easy if you are new to both the company and your position in it. No one in the room will have had sufficient exposure to you to have developed suspicions or doubts about your ability. All will be hoping for a messianic rescue of the business. If you are in this position, you might make an effective introduction by:

1. Introducing yourself personally to those whom you have not yet met.
2. Stating that you are about to embark on a turnaround program and that in order to succeed, it will require both input and output from each person present.
3. Explaining that your definition of a *turnaround* is to increase the rate of earnings to a respectable return on investment in a matter of months, and then to launch a growing, profitable enterprise from that base.
4. Advising the participants that you have not yet selected the quantitative objectives in terms of

time or dollars because you want them to play key roles in establishing specific goals.

5. Selling yourself as the person most capable of leading the turnaround, by relating your qualifications in terms of similar past accomplishments with other firms.

6. Announcing, if you are in a position to do so, the individual financial rewards that will be provided in this program (see Chapter 14).

7. Topping off with an optimistic kicker, such as "From what I've seen so far of you people and our company, I don't envision any difficulty in achieving our goal."

The introduction will be a bit more troublesome, but should follow the same format, if you have been with the company and in your current position for some time. You may have to draw on every ounce of your staff members' loyalty, and every bit of your knowledge of their individual personalities, to convince them that you are not only capable of turning over a new leaf for the company but of turning that leaf to gold. Do not say you have a foolproof new technique, and don't appeal to group empathy. These gimmicks just won't work.

If you have been with the company in your present position for some time, I recommend either of two approaches. Both require that you be away from the premises for at least two weeks immediately prior to introducing your program. Your mere absence will put a crack in the continuity of the routine you intend to break. When you return, you can extend the "Welcome back, boss" attitude of your subordinates into receptivity in welcoming the new program. Furthermore, your absence will provide you with the uninterrupted time that you need to put together your general turnaround plan.

In the first approach, prior to and during your "leave," you research or review the techniques required to implement a comprehensive turnaround program. A num-

ber of excellent executive seminars, such as those offered by the American Management Associations, and
many good books are available to meet this need. From
these learning experiences, you can devise a well thought
out program before the kickoff meeting.

In the second approach, you engage a consultant who
has helped other companies to execute successful turnarounds. Establish the ground rules together while you
are away; then introduce the consultant at the staff
meeting upon your return. Make certain to introduce
the consultant as an advisor and to leave no doubt that
you and your staff will be the doers.

If you have been with the company for some time
but are new to your position, your introductory speech
may be a little more difficult to prepare. Not only have
your weaknesses already been perceived, but some staff
members probably believe that someone else should have
been promoted to your position.

If this is your situation, I recommend that you go
ahead and stick out your neck, just as though you were
new to the company—but only after you have developed a program with which you feel confident and comfortable, and only after you have secured the full support of your immediate superior(s). I would further
suggest a preliminary review of your overall program
with a competent outside confidant.

Program Outline

The emphasis in this middle segment of the meeting
must be on selling the fact that you actually have thought
out a comprehensive program and that all members of
the staff will play major roles in its implementation.
Make sure, also, that the staff understands that the techniques you plan to use meet accepted managerial standards and have worked well for other companies. A few
specific examples will aid your cause here.

In themselves, the chapters of this book represent
steps in a program that does work well. Of course, you

should adapt and improve these steps to fit your particular situation.

Without going into great detail, outline for the members of your staff the steps you plan to take. Let them know that they, as well as other managers, will receive formal training in some of these specific techniques during the program. You might mention, as you deem advisable:

1. Establishment and attainment of short-range objectives.
2. Motivational techniques.
3. Management with objectives.
4. Strategic long-range planning.

My usual approach is to conduct the training myself so that I can retain control of the overall program. To enhance the commitment and motivation of my immediate subordinates, I send each of them to a short seminar on a different subelement of the intended project; while this is not essential, I feel it indicates to my subordinates that I am willing to invest in them and that they are a valuable part of the turnaround team. If you feel uncertain about your ability to personally conduct the training, be prepared to answer the question of who will conduct it. Numerous consultants, seminars, and training tapes are available. Allow subordinates to conduct some of their own training sessions. By doing so, you are providing motivational job enlargement—that is, incentive through added responsibilities that keep an employee working to full potential. Staff members with an aptitude for formally training others could be sent to appropriate seminars, with instructions to follow up by conducting an in-house seminar on the subject upon their return.

New Ground Rules

In order to maintain enthusiasm during the time between this announcement and meaty staff action, the meeting must have a strong closing. In addition, you must give your people something meaningful to pass on to their subordinates. The program must never be left hanging in the talking stage. Some action must commence at once, to forcefully emphasize your commitment to significant change.

I have found that the way to do this is by implementing, or reinforcing, some simple ground rules. The four ground rules that I favor are described here. They fit most company situations, a participative style of management, and the need for immediate improvement. You may find ones better suited to your style and surroundings.

1. All participants in the turnaround program must demonstrate integrity and close teamwork. Integrity goes without saying. It should be mentioned only to put it up in front of the entire program, where it must remain in order to achieve a rapid turnaround.

Teamwork is something else. Your organization is truly the exception if all your key people are already working together toward common goals to the degree necessary for a successful turnaround. Try the following story to get them started. I heard it first as a child, and it has never failed me when I wanted to dramatize a need for improved teamwork.

An old preacher friend of mine once told the story of a man who, after he had passed away, met St. Peter at the pearly gates.

"My friend," St. Peter greeted him, "because of your unusual life on earth, you are being given a choice between heaven and hell."

"Let me see hell first," the man responded. So St. Peter took him there.

The man was astounded to come upon a magnificent mansion, surrounded by beautifully landscaped gardens, complete with the splendor of flowering plants and shrubs. Wild game of every description roamed the grounds. While still awed by the exterior, the two entered the mansion. Inside everyone was seated at a huge banquet table, resplendent with delicious foods that almost defied the imagination—meats, fish, fowl, fruits, vegetables, from all corners of the universe. But all the people there seemed to be extremely depressed. Each face was ashen and haggard. They reflected extreme lack of nourishment. There wasn't a word being spoken, or a smile to be found.

"What's going on here?" asked the visitor.

"Look closely," said St. Peter.

Then the visitor noticed that all the people at the table had steel bands around both elbows, preventing them from bending their arms and getting food to their mouths. And all were chained tightly to the backs of their chairs, so they could not lean forward to get their mouths down to the food on their plates. They were unable to enjoy what they had.

"Get me out of here!" shouted the visitor. "I couldn't stand this place."

As they approached heaven, what do you think they saw? They saw an exact duplicate of the magnificent mansion and landscape they had just left—it was identical to the most minute detail. And upon entering the mansion, they viewed the same foods and smelled the same delicious aromas. But all the people at the tables were smiling and talking. They looked as healthy and happy as any group the visitor had ever seen.

"This is the place for me," he quickly observed.

"Look more closely," St. Peter replied softly.

It was then that the visitor, in utter amazement, noticed the same steel elbow bands and chair chains that he had just fled from in hell.

"Come on, St. Peter, what's the difference?" came the question.

"Here they feed each other," was St. Peter's soft reply.

They survived and found happiness only by working together.

Let your people know that they are going to be encumbered with the steel elbow bands and chair chains of learning new ways to do things and that there will be many accompanying frustrations. Let them know that despite this, you firmly believe that you and they are about to embark on an enjoyable and profitable adventure, but only if they work together, and "feed each other."

2. *All assignments must be completed on time.* Advise your subordinates that they will be assisting in establishing their own objectives and due dates throughout the program. Stress, however, that late completion of scheduled assignments will not be tolerated, except in cases where your approval has been obtained in advance. The turnaround will be vastly more difficult if you permit any after-the-fact excuses for late completion of assigned tasks. Such delinquencies will pyramid in delaying your overall program.

3. *All urgent daily problems must be resolved immediately.* This may sound ridiculous. But think about it. Once the turnaround program is under way, can you imagine anything that would be more effective in detouring it than assignments completed behind schedule and a buildup of unforeseen problems—those daily emergencies that keep throwing the ship off its charted course?

I use two techniques to push those roadblocks aside. The first came to me thirdhand and was credited to Boeing in getting its first 747 off the ground.

When Boeing was awarded its first 747 contract, it did not have a plant in which to build the plane. Yet the first 747 was in the air only one day behind schedule and that was because Seattle was socked in on the scheduled launching day.

I've been told that Boeing gives the credit for this to its "red flag" program.

From the moment ground preparation began on the vast manufacturing facility until the first 747 flew, each line supervisor was permitted a maximum of one hour to solve any problem that arose in his area. If he couldn't resolve the problem in one hour, he literally raised a red flag for his boss to see.

The red flag passed the problem up to the next level

of supervision, which was allowed two hours to solve it. All problems were passed up the chain of command in this manner, with each succeeding level of management being given twice as long to solve the problem as had been allowed to the level below it.

The president was included in this procedure, which culminated in all unresolved problems reaching the board of directors 48 hours after they first were discovered.

Implement such a "red flag" program in your organization, up to your level. At the staff meeting, ask for input on the time allowances to be granted to each level of management. Identify the positions in each level. Jointly agree on and implement the program.

The second technique I use for getting problems rapidly up to the organizational level capable of solving them is a simple practice that was the key to efficiency in the two most productive manufacturing plants I know of. It is the daily supervisors meeting, chaired by the top-ranking manufacturing manager. At such meetings, each supervisor is required to bring up any problem that is restricting performance in his or her department. Problems that can be expected to be resolved by the next meeting are specifically assigned to one person to solve by that time. Problems requiring assistance from outside the meeting group are assigned to individuals to follow up on with the appropriate parties. All problems, until resolved, remain on the meeting agenda as old business—and good supervisors do not like long meetings. Whether or not yours is a manufacturing business, if you do not already have supervisors meetings, I urge you to implement them, at least for a four-week trial.

4. *Negative statements are forbidden.* Every society has its gripers. Firms in need of a turnaround usually have more than their share of negativism because of the mistakes they have made and the condition they are in. If allowed to continue, negativism will surely impede your turnaround.

Order an immediate halt to all griping and other

negative talk by and among your key subordinates, except to you, in private. Police this elimination of negative comments softly at first, because it may require a major change in some habit patterns. And above all, set a shining example yourself.

That's it for the first step. If handled well, your turnaround is off to a flying start in the right direction. Don't forget to enforce these ground rules so that program slippage can be avoided.

2

Introduce the Program to All Other Employees

THE preceding chapter stressed the importance of involving your immediate subordinates, your key staff people, at the very beginning of a turnaround program. It is just as necessary to involve all your lower-echelon employees at this time also and to instill in them, too, a sense of enthusiastic optimism. Everyone is to be involved in the turnaround program. Its chances for success will be greatly enhanced when everyone knows the name of the game, its rules, and its progress.

Although the chain of command must be observed, and probably strengthened throughout the course of a turnaround, at times a direct oral presentation by you as the chief executive can best provide the desired effect. The start of a turnaround is one of those times.

The Kickoff Announcement

The turnaround kickoff announcement must be carefully planned with regard to employee grouping, timing, location, and content. The way that best advantage can be taken of each of these four factors will vary from company to company. The following guidelines should be amended as required to achieve maximum impact on and response from your company's people.

Employee Grouping

In most firms, the initial broad announcement of a turnaround program should be made to all members of management. This practice has merit, for if all managers are not advised in advance of their subordinates, some are certain to receive the news from peers or subordinates. That sort of communications linkage can get the program off on the wrong foot in two ways: (1) Hearing the chief executive's words for the first time from a peer or a subordinate may be a blow to a manager's need for prestige. It may lead to a bad initial attitude toward the turnaround program. (2) What that manager first hears will have already been subjected to editorial opinionizing by those passing on the information. If so, when that manager does finally hear the announcement directly from the chief executive, it will be in the weakened mode of "reaction" to already formed opinions, rather than in the stronger "action" mode that usually accompanies hearing a new thought.

A final argument for telling all managers first is that the more homogeneous the grouping, the better the meeting can promote positive participation and reaction because the leader can design all comments to fit a single group.

If the employees are unionized, it is often best to next inform the proper union committee(s). I have seen one turnaround effort temporarily foiled by union obstruction, which then immediately rotated 180 degrees to full support, merely as a result of the turnaround manager's giving slight advance notice of happenings to the local union officers.

If at all practical, the nonmanagement employees should be notified in departmental meetings of no more than 30 to 40 people. If you keep to this number, the previously mentioned advantage of homogeneity can usually be obtained.

Timing

Each turnaround program announcement meeting should be restricted to 20 to 30 minutes. In order to avoid having any employee receive the news secondhand, schedule the meetings in rapid-fire sequence. Larger organizations must consider the trade-off between the advantages of small meeting size and rapid-fire announcement. I prefer to take no more than two consecutive days to advise all employees who have even a minimal degree of daily interface with each other, and no more than a week to cover the entire organization, regardless of size. It naturally follows that to achieve this time frame in larger firms, you may need to delegate meeting leadership. If so, you have to realize that some effectiveness is usually lost with each level of delegation. So, delegation must be weighed against lengthening the announcement schedule.

Meetings should be conducted on company time with no loss of earnings or of earnings opportunity to participants. The turnaround announcement is of sufficient import to have all employees know that the company is willing to pay for it. Furthermore, if the meetings are effective, the cost will be fully recovered in 48 hours.

Location

Inconvenience your personnel and your operations as little as possible with your choice of meeting places. Refrain from selecting any environmental factors that would tend to suggest that you are making a speech. Informality, a sense of urgency, friendliness, and short meeting duration are in order.

Small departmental sit-down meetings in conference or lunch rooms work well. A stand-up meeting in a safe and quiet space within each department can also be effective. Make every effort to choose situations where all in attendance can hear your natural voice, without artificial amplification.

Content

In order to achieve a marked refreshment in employee attitudes, the content of each meeting must be carefully planned. You want to instill an attitude of enthusiastic optimism in the vast majority of employees. You can reach this objective in several ways. The remainder of this chapter discusses some of the techniques by which this may be accomplished.

In choosing what you are going to say, it is best to avoid anything that will be remembered as having been said before, as well as anything with which you feel ill at ease. Considerable impact will be lost if your people believe that they are hearing "the same old thing again" or if you seem uneasy.

Be personal. Shake hands with each employee and greet each one by name. If you aren't sure of the names of all the employees in attendance and their supervisor is present, ask the supervisor to introduce each one to you. (This requires advance notice to the supervisor in order to avoid embarrassment.) If the appropriate supervisor is not present, don't hesitate to introduce yourself to each person individually. Whenever possible, make a simple personal or job-oriented statement while shaking hands, something that can generate a short positive thought: "You're looking well. I like the way you handle that desk calculator." Something to that effect.

Most people there will want to shake your hand and will want you to show some personal awareness of them. Your short comments will help establish the positive attitude you seek.

Establish optimism. Without sounding too grim, seriously present a short outline of recent financial lowlights. Then announce (with a sincere smile) that you have called these people together to share with them your optimism about the future, based on some new plans you have that will improve the company and at the same time make each of their jobs more enjoyable and rewarding. Adjust your vocabulary as necessary to best impress each group, using language that is natural to you and understandable to your employees.

Tell your people that you are in the process of putting the finishing touches to your plans for improving the company and that you will personally see to it that they are kept informed of both changes and progress.

Explain that you know what it is like not to enjoy coming to work in the morning and that you don't want anyone in your organization to feel that way. You are going to do your best to make this company a place where people really want to work because happy employees are the keys to a healthy company.

This, by the way, is another ticket to a successful, rapid turnaround. Things tend to happen best when people enjoy making them happen. A well-managed turnaround program will provide the recognition, job understanding, job enrichment opportunities, and discipline that generate employee enthusiasm.

Encourage teamwork. Emphasize the high priority that you place on teamwork, and the importance of each job to the overall success of the organization. (Use an actual example or two, applicable to that group, of how each job supports the whole.)

Explain why and how clients or customers are the sole source of funds for all wages and salaries, and how conditions may improve for each one of them in almost direct proportion to the increase in the number of satisfied clients/customers. Then drive home your point with examples of how performance in any one job can gain or lose a client/customer.

Let your people know that they are in direct competition with their counterparts at similar companies in the industry and that you will be taking a personal interest in what each one of them is doing to give clients what they expect, when they expect it, in a better way than any of their competitors do. For example, if you are addressing an assembly department, remind them that their competitors all have assembly employees and that customers will give the most new orders to the assembly department that does the best job. You might use a sports analogy of championships going to the best team.

Show your grasp of detail. Getting back to the advantage of having employees feel that you are personally interested in them, it would be fitting to reemphasize that your ivory tower is not so far removed from them as they might imagine.

Avoid the statement frequently used by executives to stress their similarity to lower-echelon personnel: "We really aren't so different. In the morning I put my trousers on one leg at a time, just like you do." It is difficult to use that old saw without implying superiority or, at least, difference. I'm reminded of the coach of a small college basketball team that was about to play the University of Kentucky, then top ranked and much taller. He advised his players that their forthcoming opponents were not that different in that they too put their sweatsuits on one leg at a time. His point was turned against him when one of his players reminded the team that Kentucky wore much more expensive sweatsuits and took much longer to pull them up those lengthy legs.

Instead, use this opportunity to gain respect for your awareness of everyday happenings in each department. Many of your personnel believe that you have no idea of what really takes place at their jobs. A quick walk through each department at any time during the week prior to the employee meeting will provide you with sufficient firsthand observations to point out specific pluses and minuses in its operations. Select one or two examples that the participants would not expect you to recognize. Surprise them with your compliments, criticisms, and specific suggestions for rapid improvements that they can make on their own. Be careful to do this in a manner that will not offend the departmental supervisors.

You can bet that most of your suggested improvements will be made in short order and that talk at many family dinner tables that evening will include complimentary references to the boss.

Say thank you. Tell the group that you are proud of them and that you know they are doing a good job. Don't hesitate to add that you won't rest until what is good becomes better and what is better becomes best. Thank them for their performance and for their attention at the meeting.

If there is time, you might solicit questions. But be careful; frequently, such an invitation leads to either an extended gripe session or the need to cut off an employee who wishes to say something. The turnaround executive who is not adept at handling such situations should forgo this.

Whether or not the meeting is opened to questions from the floor, it is very important to encourage the members of each group to feel free to question their supervisors about the meeting and the turnaround program. Reinforce your commitment to keep them well informed.

Comment on future communications. Close the meeting by repeating to the participants that you will see to it that they will be among the first to know of future changes and progress.

If these meetings have been conducted properly, the turnaround bandwagon will gain many riders because your employees will believe in your ability to get that wagon where they think it should go and because they expect to enjoy the trip.

3
Take a Financial Inventory

PICTURE a 5'7" basketball player making a slam dunk from midcourt in the opposing team's basket. Ridiculous? Of course.

That is why a business turnaround, like any other activity involving goals, must start with a sound assessment of present conditions. Who are we as a company or department (what is our stated mission)? Where are we now? Where are we heading? Let's not make a move until we are certain of who and where we are!

With total commitment from the top line executive, such an evaluation can be completed in three to six weeks, depending on the size and nature of the enterprise. It consists of at least these five parts:

1. An inventory of current financial strengths, weaknesses, and trends.
2. An audit of the performance level of each management function.
3. An evaluation of each key employee in the organization.
4. Input from each key employee on needs, problems, and opportunities.
5. A preliminary listing of problems and opportunities to be attacked first on a short-range basis.

The primary objective of a business turnaround is

usually to regain financial strength. Therefore, an analysis of current financial conditions should be the first step in the assessment process.

There are two other reasons for giving top priority to the balance sheet, the income statement, and supportive reports. While most successful turnarounds require only minimal funding, some infusion of cash is frequently required. A sound grasp of the present financial situation will provide valuable information concerning sources and limitations of this potentially necessary resource.

The third reason for beginning in this manner comes from my personal observations of a number of turnaround attempts. Turnarounds are most successful when they are aimed solely at improving return on investment. This target demands an accurate, high-powered rifle with its sight always trained on the bull's-eye.

Perhaps, like me, you have witnessed turnaround or rapid earnings growth programs that zeroed in on an excellent marketing scheme, a new service or product, a productivity improvement concept, or even "better communication." An adequate progress reporting system was put into effect; regular management meetings assured the "success" of the program; and months later, someone higher up in the organization asked why the results of the program could not be found in the income statement. Such a scenario is not uncommon.

Your turnaround program must focus intently on improving return on assets employed, and its results must be readily identifiable in your regular financial reporting. Therefore, the success of a turnaround program is greatly enhanced when: (1) you share financial results with all key people involved and (2) those key people perceive you, their leader, to be a financial expert.

In order to achieve this perception in your key people, you must (1) maintain a strong grasp on the meaning of all pertinent financial data and (2) report the data and discuss their meaning directly with your immediate staff.

How many times have you heard a chief line executive state or imply at the beginning of a meeting, "Now it is time for us to hear from our chief financial officer with the monthly financial report," and after that report has been given, "Thank you, Terry. Now let's get down to the real reason for this meeting." This statement submerges the significance of financial performance when, in fact, the financial picture is of utmost importance and should be stressed rather than deemphasized.

If your subordinates feel you have a keen eye for financial data and an insatiable appetite for improved return of investment, most of them will automatically direct their senses of sight and taste in those directions, to the benefit of your turnaround program.

The Financial Inventory

Again, the purposes of the financial inventory are to identify both the glaring and subtle financial strengths and weaknesses and to impress your staff with your financial expertise.

The analysis need not be exhaustive and can be performed in the detail required by most accounting personnel. In some cases, the data may already be available, or they may be readily attainable in print-out form from data processing.

In order to identify trends, some historical period and frequency must be decided upon. A good rule of thumb is to evaluate at least the past five years on an annual basis and the past two years on a monthly basis. However, there are exceptions. Return on investment, for example, is seldom meaningful on a monthly basis, but it is usually meaningful on a quarterly basis. Being such an important indicator, ROI should be traced for at least five years in the shortest meaningful intervals.

Often, changes in accounting procedures over the years make it almost impossible to make worthwhile historical comparisons. It is important that you identify the effects of such procedural changes, so that viable trends can be portrayed. But it is even more important that you not compare apples with oranges. On this point, remember also that it is invalid to compare two trends that were established over different time periods. For example, an annual increase of 10 percent in sales over the past ten years should not be compared with an annual decline of 1 percent in earnings over the past five years. Each of these trends may be significant when taken alone, but together they have little mathematical substance.

A convenient means for presenting the collected data is shown in Figure 1. Both regular and semilog graph paper are used to show trends in absolute and percentage terms. However, most trends can be adequately presented by the use of only one of the two graphs. Note that two trend lines are shown on each graph. The solid line is a least-squares fit to each datum point. The broken line is also a least-squares fit, but it excludes the effect of any datum point more than 1.7 standard deviations from the original trend line, thus eliminating the influence of extremely abnormal circumstances.

The factors that should be analyzed by most companies in need of a turnaround are taken from the balance sheet, the income statement, and supportive reports.

The Balance Sheet

Although this extremely important document merits at least as much attention and comprehension as the income statement, many operating executives tend to shy away from it. To do so is a mistake. I have seen several cases where the personal efforts of the chief executive were required to obtain necessary funds at a good price from financial institutions. In each instance, the chief executive's knowledge of the company's balance sheet was a decisive factor in determining the cost of borrowed funds. The more comfortable a chief execu-

Figure 1. ZAB Corporation—annual net sales (in millions of dollars).

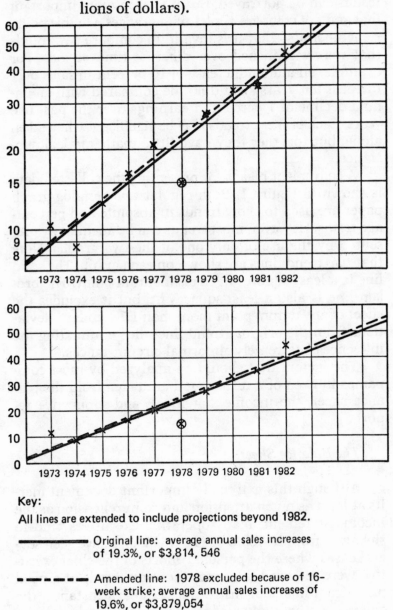

Key:

All lines are extended to include projections beyond 1982.

———————— Original line: average annual sales increases of 19.3%, or $3,814, 546

– – – – – – Amended line: 1978 excluded because of 16-week strike; average annual sales increases of 19.6%, or $3,879,054

Benchmark for comparison: industry-wide average annual sales increases of 21.3% for the same period

tive was in discussing and projecting the balance sheet without input from the company's accountants, the better were the terms of the loan. The chief executive's ability to discuss and project the company's income statement seemed to have little or no influence.

Analyze the following elements from the balance sheet:

$$1. \text{ Current ratio} = \frac{\text{current assets}}{\text{current liabilities}}$$

A current ratio of 2:1 is usually considered healthy. A ratio of much less than that often can lead to problems in meeting current liabilities. A ratio much higher than 2.5:1 could mean idle working capital.

$$2. \text{ Acid-test ratio} = \frac{\text{current assets} - \text{inventories}}{\text{current liabilities}}$$

A fair yardstick here is a ratio of 1.5:1. A ratio of less than 1:1 is frequently dangerous; a ratio above 2:1 may indicate idle working capital.

$$3. \text{ Cash ratio} = \frac{\text{cash}}{\text{current liabilities}}$$

A cash ratio of from 0.7:1 to 1:1 is considered healthy. Less is dangerous; much more suggests the need to determine whether cash is being invested advantageously.

4. Fixed asset growth

At what rates have the gross and net values of fixed assets been increasing? How steady are these rates of growth? Average annual growth rates of less than 10 percent indicate no real growth at all. Annual growth rates in excess of 30 percent suggest a need to take a hard look at the control reporting system, for such rapid growth rates often require especially strong control reporting to prevent them from getting out of hand.

5. Debt

At what rates have debt and lease obligations been growing? What future obligations exist with respect to principal and interest? Do recent earnings trends indicate any past or future problems in meeting debt obligations? Debt should probably be growing but at a slower rate than either assets or equity, unless there is a strong reason to support the contrary. Compare growth of debt to growth of net fixed assets and equity in order to assure that debt has been used to expand the business.

The Income Statement

In contrast to their attitude toward balance sheets, most executives have a reasonable amount of confidence in their ability to interpret their company's income statements. Once again the executive can demonstrate to his staff that he, unlike most other executives, comprehends the subtleties of this financial report. Analysis of the following elements from the income statement will help you to better understand its implications:

6. Sales

At what rates have gross and net sales been growing? Has the growth been consistent? Are there any definite seasonal patterns? The sales growth rates should exceed the rate of growth of the economy in general, of the industry in which the company competes, and of the balance-sheet items just noted. Again, growth rates of less than 10 percent a year spell oncoming doom, for they represent no growth at all, and growth rates in excess of 30 percent indicate a need for strong controls to prevent the speed of growth from exceeding management's ability to control it properly.

7. Earnings

At what rates have pretax and net earnings grown? Have they kept pace with sales, assets, and debt? What has been the monthly history of pretax earnings as a percentage of sales?

8. Budget column

The internal income statement should note the amount budgeted for each key line item. What have been the trends of performance to budget?

9. Discounts, returns, allowances

If the company gives discounts from list or base prices, credit for customer complaints or returns, or cash discounts amounting to more than 1 percent, it is well to segregate them and report them as such on the income statement. A typical example might be:

Sales at list	$4,000
Standard discounts	2,000
Special discounts	100
Special premiums	50
Gross sales	$1,950
Returns	12
Cash discounts	6
Net sales	$1,932

Analyze the trends in these line items to the degree that they have been segregated in prior reports.

10. Material, labor, overhead

What has been the trend in material costs as a percentage of net sales? By major department or function, what have been the trends in labor and overhead as percentages of net sales? These are numbers well worth remembering. When your subordinates know that you know and remember what they are spending, they make it a point to keep it in their minds as well. By so doing, they tend to spend more carefully.

11. Major cost elements

Which elements of cost account for more than 10 percent of net sales? For more than 5 percent? For more than 2 percent? What have been their trends? These items are prime areas for cost reduction.

12. Variances from standard costs

If your company has a standard cost system, what have been the trends in variances from standard costs? Which variances have been the largest? Because very few companies in need of a turnaround have good standard cost systems, the variances here should be suspect. Even so, it is useful to have some knowledge of them.

13. Break-even point analysis
Here is the formula for figuring the break-even point.

Break-even point = fixed expenses for the period ÷

$$\left(1 - \frac{\text{variable expenses for the period}}{\text{sales for the period}}\right)$$

If a break-even point analysis is not part of your regular financial package, institute one. Have a projected profit/volume graph drawn up to discuss with your staff. (See Figure 2.) Or, if this is not possible, at least have a break-even point analysis made for prior periods to show historical trends.

The Combined Income Statement and Balance Sheet

Some important financial ratios require the use of data from both the balance sheet and the income statement.

14. Return on assets
This is the most critical financial ratio for most chief operating executives. Check individual ratios and their trend. An annualized pretax return of 25 to 35 percent is sound. Although very high returns are desirable, long-run returns in excess of 40 percent tend to invite a high degree of new competition and, eventually, excess industry-wide capacity.

15. Collection period for accounts receivable
The number of days of receivables outstanding should be reported monthly as a regular part of your financial package. Target figures vary greatly from industry to industry. Your number of days outstanding should be below the average for your type of business. Trend is very important. Both customer satisfaction and credit management must be excellent so that your number of days does not increase sharply when money is in tight supply.

16. Payment period for accounts payable
What has been the trend in the number of days of payables outstanding? Have you been operating with your vendors' money to the maximum extent possible with-

Figure 2. ZAB Corporation—break-even point analysis.

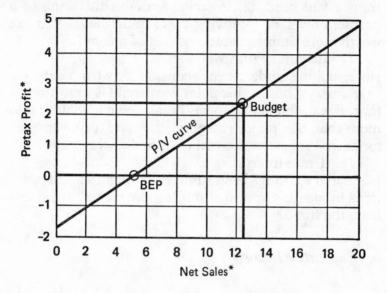

Per First-Quarter Budget for Next Year[†]
Net Sales = $12,500

	Costs		
	Total	Fixed	Variable
Materials	$ 4,132	$	$4,123
Direct Labor	1,519	130	1,389
Manufacturing Overhead	1,997	390	1,607
Selling & Distribution	1,497	450	1,047
General & Other Expenses	998	800	198
TOTAL	$10,134	$1,770	$8,364

$$BEP = 1{,}770 \div \left(1 - \frac{8{,}364}{12{,}500}\right) = \frac{1{,}770}{0.331} = \$5{,}347$$

*000,000 omitted.
[†]000 omitted.

out: (1) damaging your ability to get the quality and service you need, (2) lowering your credit rating to a problem level, or (3) giving up cash discounts that are worth more than your present cost of money?

17. Inventory turnover

Here, again, standards vary considerably from industry to industry. Thus at this point your trend is most important. If your financial reports break down inventory into more than one major category, calculate turnover rates for each. Which rates are highest and lowest?

18. Times interest earned

Have your earnings been sufficiently high to avoid problems in meeting specified interest payments? What has been the trend?

Supportive Reports

As mentioned earlier, all monthly financial packages should include supportive control reports. Some worth having and reviewing at this point are:

19. Incoming business, production, shipments, backlog

What is the current situation? How much work is there in the present backlog? What has been the recent history? Do new orders and shipments flow in the same pattern? If not, how do the patterns differ?

If your company does not already have one, immediately set up a weekly report of incoming orders, production, shipments, and backlog.

20. Sources and applications of funds

What have the sources of money coming into your business been? For what have earnings been used? What percentage of earnings has been reinvested in the business? What are the trends?

21. Sales and earnings by product line

What have the sales trends of the most and least profitable lines been? What questions do these data raise?

22. Sales and earnings by geographic area

23. Sales and earnings by salesperson or group

24. Complete and on-time delivery performance
What percentage of your orders has been delivered complete and on time? What are the trends? Better than 90 percent is usually required for adequate market credibility.

25. Quality performance
What measures of quality are now routinely reported? Are they adequate and meaningful? What are the levels of rejects and customer complaints? What have been their trends?

26. Costs of key commodities
What are your key raw materials? What have the recent trends in their unit costs been?

27. Staffing
What is your employment in total and in terms of meaningful subgroups, such as direct labor, factory interest, marketing, and so forth? What are the current turnover rates? What have the trends in employment and turnover been?

28. Sales and earnings per employee
This is a very meaningful statistic that should be reported regularly. What are the trends here?

29. Assets per employee
What has been the trend in the cost of providing a job for one person?

30. Capital budget
Does a formal capital budget exist, and is activity reported on a regular monthly basis? What are the immediate plans for capital investment? How much has already been committed? Have past returns on investment been as budgeted?

31. Physical inventory
How frequently are physical inventories taken? How has physical inventory compared to book inventory recently? Have the differences been relatively consistent? It is worth noting here that it is not unusual for a new operating executive to inherit an inventory shortage surprise in a marginal or declining company.

Using the Financial Inventory

In addition to providing you with an excellent grasp of the financial and accounting side of your business, the completed financial inventory will serve several other very useful purposes.

It will identify areas that need attention in the short- and long-range plans that must be developed soon. (These plans are described in Chapters 9 and 13.) In that it quantifies many elements of the enterprise, the completed inventory can also be used to estimate the potential returns from various courses of corrective action. Thus it will serve as a basis for selecting and setting priorities for strategies and objectives.

Also, the completed inventory should uncover meaningless, misleading, and unnecessary control reports. Of even greater importance is information that is needed on a regular basis but that has not been forthcoming. Systems must be implemented at once to ensure regular, accurate reporting of all needed information.

Finally, the completed inventory provides a worthwhile agenda for a staff meeting. Such meetings are of fundamental importance to the success of a turnaround. They foster and maintain enthusiasm and direct both conscious and subconscious attention to the project.

A dual-purpose staff meeting is recommended. Use the meeting first to impress your immediate subordinates with your financial acumen. Take several of the inventory summary sheets that illustrate greatest strengths and weaknesses and discuss them with your staff, emphasizing the financial and stockholder viewpoints. Make certain not to discuss items about which your limited knowledge causes you to feel uncomfortable.

Then discuss shortcomings of your control reporting system. Solicit comments and recommendations for additions, deletions, and modifications.

Sources of Funds

The major point to be made on the subject of cash availability is that acquisition of additional cash, if needed, should be the easiest step in the turnaround program. Although a discussion of the pros and cons of alternative sources of funds is beyond the scope of this book, a word of caution is in order.

Be patient. Avoid taking irrevocable steps to obtain additional cash until you have: (1) established your business integrity, (2) talked with your bankers, key customers, and vendors, and (3) developed your long-range strategic plan.

Allow a little time for the word to circulate from your employees and customers that there has indeed been a change for the better—a change appreciated by both insiders and outsiders.

Meet separately with executive contacts at your bank(s), key customers, and key vendors (see Chapter 7). Take time to impress them with your knowledge of the business as it relates to their individual interests, as well as with your sincere desire to respond to those interests as long as it can be mutually beneficial. Convince these contacts that a noteworthy improvement has taken place in your company. If possible, demonstrate your integrity by making some specific short-range commitments you are certain to keep. Even minor commitments, when met, can be meaningful. These contacts, who may know of some sources for funds of which you are unaware, could become a valuable financial reference for your company—even through casual comments they make to fellow golfers at the nineteenth hole of the local country club.

Most important, prepare your long-range strategic plan (Chapter 13) before seeking any outside funds. A good strategic plan can help you obtain funds in at least two ways. First, it will provide a much more accurate picture of the total funds needed, of the funds that will be generated internally, and of the rate at which any debt might be retired. Second, a well-presented strategic plan can be instrumental in reducing the cost of funds, by being a most effective tool in selling your company to prospective creditors.

4
Audit Each Function of the Business

ALL the evaluation processes suggested in this book are intended to provide you with a multidimensional evaluation of your business, in order to strengthen your ability to select and set priorities for the best future strategies and objectives. This particular step in the turnaround process requires you to systematically evaluate the current performance level of the functions within your company or department that are most responsible for business success or failure.

The functional audit serves several purposes. First, it assures a comprehensive search for problem areas, as well as for pockets of strength. Just as some companies tend to get into ruts, some managers have been concerned about one problem for so long that their thinking has become locked in to it, as if it were the only serious problem they have. Frequently, there are other, sometimes underlying, problems that merit equal or greater attention. Managers also tend to be biased either for or against the functional areas in which they have the greatest expertise.

The case of a general manager whose forte is sales and marketing is a good example. His special knowledge of that function will impose a bias in his treatment of its performance. Depending on other factors, he often will operate unknowingly from that bias by being either overly demanding or overly protective of the Sales and Marketing functions. The same pattern frequently holds for areas about which the manager knows the least. And unfortunately there are managers who have never even initiated a search for the sick trees in their woods. The functional audit forces that search to be made.

Second, the functional audit provides an effective learning tool for many managers, even though it may be only a refresher course. In performing the audit, you personally look into the nooks and crannies of each function of your business, in terms of both the supportive actions that should be performed and the current level of their execution. This process produces new thoughts as well as recollection of valuable old thoughts. The functional audit is also a particularly useful learning device for new managers, since it provides them with a quick grasp of their inheritance.

Third, the functional audit provides a necessary foundation for the turnaround steps discussed in Chapter 8. That chapter sets forth ways for you to solicit business problems and opportunities from your subordinates. By personally completing this audit, you will be better prepared to evaluate suggestions from your staff. Furthermore, by discussing your audit findings with the respective functional head after the audit, you better equip each one for offering input at a later stage.

Finally, the functional audit usually uncovers some problems that can be remedied on the spot, thus permitting you to shift the turnaround program into a higher gear.

A typical list of functions and subfunctions for a manufacturing company is included at the end of this chapter. Select the ones that apply to your business or department; add others that you deem pertinent to your circumstances. For each function, list the elements critical to its success and the questions pertinent to each element (see Figure 3). Leave some blank space at the end of each function to accommodate pertinent suggestions regarding that function from your subordinates.

Then complete the rating sheets: First, write in a comment on the right-hand side for each item on the left, and then subjectively rate each item on a scale of 0 to 10. Do this, step by step, only as you feel reasonably satisfied with your knowledge of each item. Some personal investigations on your part almost certainly will be necessary. After you have rated the critical elements for a function, select an overall rating of 0 to 10 for that function as a whole but do not write it in. Then calculate the arithmetic mean of the critical element ratings. If your overall rating is the same as the mean or differs from it by not more than one rating point, enter either of the two numbers under the rating column for the total function. If your overall rating differs from the mean by more than one point, reconsider the critical element ratings as well as the overall rating and reconcile them so that the difference is not more than one rating point. Then record either of the two numbers in the rating column for the total function. In the bottom section of the figure that you used to write subordinates' suggestions, also note the reasoning process by which you arrived at this total.

After you have audited all functions, meet individually with your immediate subordinate in charge of each function. Discuss your opinions with that person, without divulging your numerical ratings. Ask each functional head for 0-to-10 ratings during the discussion. Attempt to reach near agreement on each point, and modify your comments and numbers accordingly.

Complete the summary forms shown in Figures 4 and 5. The completed forms may require further adjustment from added information, which will be forthcoming in later steps of the preparatory process.

The finished audit will then serve as one of the foundations for short- and long-range objectives, strategies, and tasks. All areas of strength deserve consideration for exploitation. All areas of weakness, for correction.

This audit also serves as a useful tool for an annual review of progress. By checking it once a year, you will be able to spot improvements that otherwise might have been overlooked. This will provide you with a few feath-

Figure 3. Functional audit rating sheet.

Sales and Marketing Function

Critical Elements	Rating
1. The degree to which the Sales and Marketing function successfully markets itself.	8
a. Are there regular, formal customer surveys and follow–up actions? Results? Trends?	9
b. Are unsolicited customer remarks logged and followed up? Results? Trends?	3
. .	
k. What is the company–wide level of respect for the Sales and Marketing function?	8
2. The level of delivery integrity a.	8

.
    .
    .
    f.	

3. The presence of a sound, formal strategic marketing plan. a.	9

.
    .
    .
    i.	

4. The degree to which sales and marketing per- sonnel understand and respect their relationships with Engineering and Production. a.	5

.
    .
    .
    f.	

5. The adequacy of sales and marketing control reports. a.	8

.
    .
    .
    f.	

TOTAL SALES AND MARKETING	8
Suggestions:	

Comments
Excellent per customer feedback except customer service response to order status inquiries.
Regular questionnaires sent every April. 50% response. "Very good" rating. Trend is good.
Logging slipshod. Follow-up hit and miss. Need to assign responsibility.
Highly respected. Some flack on pressures for special delivery requests from Denver rep.
92% complete and on time. Quality very good per survey. Up from 70% two years ago. Shop committed.
Excellent plan in effect and ahead of schedule. Good forecasts. Know competition.
Not enough documentation of sales estimates and design parameters for new products. Sales tries to bypass channels for product change.
Minimal, but effective. Dedicated to improve reported data.

Figure 4. Functional audit summary form for ratings.

Private Functional Audit Summary

Function	Rating	Comments
Sales and Marketing	8	Excellent by industry
Markets itself	8	standards. Must improve
Delivery integrity	8	customer service and for-
Performance to plan	9	malize procedures govern-
Interfunctional respect	5	ing product change. Evaluate
Adequacy of controls	8	Denver sales rep.
Product Engineering (R&D)		
Bills of material		
Interfunctional respect		
Performance to plan		
Adequacy of controls		
Production		
Delivery integrity		
Productivity		
Performance to plan		
Adequacy of controls		
Materials Management		
Bills of material, etc.		
Overall control system		
Everything in place		
Transaction reporting		
Respect from production		
Performance to plan		
Adequacy of controls		
Manufacturing Engineering		
Savings ratio		
Respect from production		
Performance to plan		
Adequacy of controls		
Quality Assurance		
Comprehension of purpose		
Quality improvement		
Performance ot plan		
Adequacy of controls		
Finance and Accounting		
Contribution to earnings		
No surprises		
Performance to plan		
Adequacy of controls		
Personnel		
Hiring success		
Welfare of individuals		
Performance to plan		
Adequacy of controls		
Mgmt. Information Services		
Response level		
Knowledge of its field		
Performance to plan		
Adequacy of controls		

ers in your managerial achievement cap that aren't readily apparent in the regular financial statements and that you may wish to comment on in reporting progress. In addition, an annual review will aid in identifying new opportunities in areas that have slipped back in relation to others. Hopefully, you won't find any factors where the slippage has been absolute.

Functions and Subfunctions to Be Audited in a Manufacturing Company

The functions and subfunctions discussed in this section are typical for most manufacturing companies. They are presented as a direct aid to readers in manufacturing businesses and as an example of format and thoroughness to readers who are not. Before beginning your audit, list the key functions in your organization. Under each, note the elements most critical to the success of that function. Below each element jot down as many pertinent questions as you can.

The Sales and Marketing Function

Excluding the products themselves (which will be audited under Product Engineering), five interrelated items are critical to the strength of the Sales and Marketing function: (1) the degree to which the Sales and Marketing function successfully markets itself, (2) the level of delivery integrity, (3) the soundness of a formal strategic marketing plan, (4) the degree to which sales and marketing personnel understand and respect the relationships among their function and the Engineering and Production functions, and (5) the adequacy of sales and marketing control reports.

1. The degree to which the Sales and Marketing function successfully markets itself. In many businesses, the level of customer respect for the Marketing function it-

Figure 5. Functional audit summary form for strengths and needs.

Functional Audit Summary

Function	Major Strengths	Greatest Needs
Sales and Marketing		
Product Engineering (R&D)		
Production		
Materials Management		
Manufacturing/ Process Engineering		
Quality Assurance		
Finance and Accounting		
Personnel		
Management Information Services		
OVERALL COMPANY		

self, including its sales representatives, accounts for more than half the decision to buy, or not to buy, their product. The other half of that decision relates to the product or service itself and the price at which it is offered.

a. Are there regular, formal customer surveys and follow-up actions? What have been the results? The trends?
b. Are unsolicited customer remarks logged and followed up? What have been the results? The trends?
c. How effective is the sales force? It is the best type? Is its organization sound? How effective is the performance of individual personnel?
d. What is the level of professionalism at the sales desk or in customer service department(s)? Are call-back promises kept?
e. What is the personal integrity level of key sales and marketing personnel?
f. What is the motivational level of the Sales and Marketing organization as a whole? Of key individuals?
g. How effective is advertising? Are the most effective types being used? Are unique strengths being promoted? Is the advertising credible? Compelling? Cost-effective?
h. How sound are prices, pricing policies and actions, terms, and freight billings? How frequently do they change? Are they competitive? Is your firm a leader or a follower? Are they respected by customers?
i. Are sales closed with speed and authority?
j. Is there a strong corporate identity program?
k. What is the company-wide level of respect for the Sales and Marketing function?

2. *The level of delivery integrity.* Getting the customers what they expect when they expect it at least 95 percent of the time is often a distinct competitive advantage and frequently carries with it an unrecognized cost-reduction bonus. Lack of delivery integrity is a weakness common

to most manufacturing concerns in need of a turn-around. The profit loss from poor delivery is not always a result of sales lost to competitors with better delivery performance. More often, it results from the tremendous costs that late-order follow-up imposes on each and every department.

a. Are orders entered and processed as rapidly and as accurately as possible?
b. Are delivery lead times competitive? Satisfactory to the customer?
c. Are in-plant personnel totally committed to the sanctity of the customer or shop order?
d. What is the level of field service performance? Response time? Integrity of work?
e. Is there adequate planning and control for problem orders?
f. Does factory supervision understand and appreciate that complete and on-time deliveries are one of the most effective cost-reduction tools?

3. The presence of a sound formal strategic marketing plan. Studies have shown that long-range business successes correlate more highly with a company's formal strategic planning effort than with any other factor.

a. Does the company have a viable mission statement?
b. Is there a formal definition of customers' wants and needs?
c. Is there an up-to-date analysis of competitors, listing your strategies versus theirs, your strengths versus theirs, your weaknesses versus theirs?
d. Is there a formal plan to capitalize on your strengths and their weaknesses? To eliminate your weaknesses?
e. Are market trends formally and accurately plotted? What is your share of market? Are there formal plans to increase penetration?

f. Have your sales forecasts been reliable? Who has been your most reliable forecaster?

g. Has there been a formal evaluation of anticipated effects of external factors, such as energy, electronics, government, the economy?

h. Are you in compliance with all fair trade and antitrust laws and regulations?

i. Is there a formal contingency plan(s)?

4. *The degree to which sales and marketing personnel understand and respect the relationships among their function and the Engineering and Production functions.* A number of companies have collapsed because sales and marketing personnel have failed to recognize both the need for carefully documented product engineering and the fact that the Production battleship cannot change course with the speed of the Sales torpedo boat.

a. What do your product engineers think of the Sales and Marketing function?

b. What do your manufacturing managers think of the Sales and Marketing function?

c. What do sales and marketing managers think of the Engineering and Production functions?

5. *The adequacy of sales and marketing control reports.* You can't get to where you plan to go if you don't know where you are now and the direction in which you are heading. Action plans are of little value without schedules and goals and a means for measuring performance against them. Are the following measured regularly and effectively:

a. Sales to budget or forecast?

b. Expenses to budget and sales?

c. On-time and complete delivery percentages?

d. Accuracy of forecasts?

e. Sales to quota for each salesperson?

f. Effectiveness of salespeople's itineraries?

g. Customer discounts and allowances?

    h. Profit/cost ratio for each sales representative?
    i. Profit/cost ratio for each geographical market area?
    j. Cost-effectiveness of distribution?
    k. Customer complaints and compliments?
    l. Freight and installation damages?
    m. Complaint reaction time?
    n. Back orders/short shipments?
    o. Service calls?
    p. Order entry time and accuracy?
    q. Response time on parts orders?

The Product Engineering Function

I want to make two points before outlining this section of the audit. First, you must have a solid working knowledge of your product offerings. If you are new and don't know your products, you must learn them post-haste, by the numbers, if that is a common form of reference. Second, as noted earlier, strong R&D/product engineering is of little value without strong marketing—competitors with stronger marketing functions and/or a major market share will find the means to pirate and sell your ideas.

In addition to the basic need for capable personnel (which applies to every function), four factors are critical to the performance of Product Engineering: (1) accurate, up-to-date bills of material in a form that best meets overall company needs, (2) a strong interface between Product Engineering, Marketing, and Production, (3) a sound, formal strategic product engineering plan, and (4) adequate product engineering control reports.

1. Accurate, up-to-date bills of material in a form that best meets overall company needs. A lack of appreciation for and commitment to clean bills of material has been a major contributor to the failure of many companies engaged in the production of assembled products.

a. Are the bills of material current and immediately updated to reflect all applicable changes?
b. Is the accuracy level of bills of material above 99 percent?
c. Are the bills of material constructed in a form that best serves the combined needs of Production, Engineering, Marketing, Accounting, Management Information Systems (MIS)?
d. Does Production comply with bills of material 100 percent of the time, except for duly authorized deviations?

2. *A strong, cooperative interface between Product Engineering, Marketing, and Production.* A strong, concerted effort by these three functions, including Accounting at times, is essential to successful product engineering.

a. Are there regular product review meetings with representation from each of the functions noted above?
b. Is there a formal program to remove low-volume and low-profit products?
c. Do the above functions participate in regular reviews of customer wants and needs, market trends and developments, competitor offerings?
d. What are the levels of aggressiveness and coordination in eliminating product weaknesses?
e. Is the rate of product change within the cost-effective capability of Production to absorb it?
f. How are production limitations (tolerances, alloying, scrap, lost time, methods, etc.) considered in product design? Is Product Engineering properly involved in process and equipment changes, as needed to comply with design changes? What is the level of Marketing and Production veto power on product designs and design changes?
g. Are responsibilities properly assigned, and is interdepartmental cooperation at a satisfactory level

in implementing product change, including pilot runs?

h. Is the cost for product engineering of "special" orders being charged to the proper account(s)?

i. What is the level of company-wide respect for the Product Engineering function?

3. *A sound, formal strategic product engineering plan.* Such a company-wide strategic plan is a necessity. The degree to which all functions are included in it, and perform to it, is critical to its success.

a. Is there documentation of where products stand in their life cycle?

b. Are new and changed products formally planned sufficiently in advance?

c. Are new and changed products compatible with company mission and strategies?

d. Do product designs meet government and industry safety standards?

4. *Adequate product engineering control reports.* A limited number of control reports are necessary to measure performance to goals, to control product quality, and to safeguard against product liability claims.

a. Are there formal documents approved and adhered to by Marketing, Product Engineering, Production, and Accounting covering all new and significantly changed products? Do they specify models, sales volume projections, estimated costs, and prices? Is enforcement rigorous?

b. Is every product change properly authorized by formal document?

c. When needed, are temporary deviations from standard specifications for a specific number of "problem" units properly authorized by formal document?

d. Are design projects scheduled, and is performance to schedule measured regularly?

e. Is product documentation sufficient to provide protection in case of product liability claims?

The Production Function

Four factors are critical to the strength of the Production function: (1) delivery integrity, (2) productivity, (3) performance to a sound, formal strategic plan, and (4) adequate production control reports.

Three other functions, closely related to the Production function, will be evaluated separately in a later section. They are Material Control, Manufacturing/Process Engineering, and Quality Assurance.

1. Delivery integrity. The primary responsibility of the Production function must be to make all products to specification on schedule.

a. Do production supervisors meet daily with the superintendent to resolve immediate problems?

b. Is there sufficient advance review of problem orders?

c. What is the degree of adherence to bills of material? Routings? Process sheets? Are all deviations authorized in advance by Product Engineering?

d. What are production delays costing in dollars and employee frustrations? Is all material at work centers when needed? Is material easily processed? Do all parts fit? Does equipment function properly?

e. To what degree do production employees understand and respect their relationship to customers? Is there absolute respect for the customer/shop order?

f. Are problems solved at the lowest effective level of management? Do unsolved problems rise to that level rapidly enough?

g. Do production supervisors have sufficient understanding of product liability?

2. Productivity. Although this factor is often associated only with direct labor, it should be understood by all managers to mean the dollar value of good output divided by total dollar input. A strong Production organization usually has a record of steadily increasing productivity.

   a. What is the attitude of production supervisors and hourly employees toward productivity?

   b. If there is union activity, is it aiding or impairing productivity?

   c. Are start, stop, and break times adequately enforced?

   d. Is there a concentrated effort to minimize time spent in tasks other than those that directly add value to the product?

   e. Is overtime properly authorized and controlled?

   f. Is housekeeping very good to excellent? Are there problem areas?

   g. Is energy conservation formally enforced?

   h. What is the efficiency level of materials handling?

   i. Does the work flow in reasonably straight lines?

   j. Is scrap/rework controlled at a satisfactory level? Are rework turnaround times acceptable? What have been the recent trends in rework turnaround times? Is defective work charged to the department/work center at fault?

   k. Is the interference level of scheduled spare parts and small special orders acceptable?

   l. Do all production supervisors have positive, motivational attitudes toward their subordinate hourly employees?

   m. What is the age and condition of buildings and equipment?

   n. Are the number of production supervisors and levels of production supervision cost-effective?

   o. What level of influence does Production have in reducing the costs of new and changed products while they are still in the planning stage?

   p. What percentage of supervisors' time is spent in the activity of supervising? Are individual supervisors devoting too much or too little time to planning, setup, engineering, or other tasks?

q. Do production supervisors accept the responsibility for inventory, and for taking regular periodic physical inventories, as an important element of their jobs?

r. If hourly employees are paid on an incentive basis, how effective is the program?

s. What is the level of cooperation within the Production function? Is there buck-passing?

t. Do production supervisors and hourly employees have acceptable attitudes toward product quality?

3. *Performance to a sound, formal strategic plan.*

a. Are facilities on schedule with the plan?
b. Are capacities according to plan?
c. Is there a formal evaluation of the anticipated effects of external influences: Energy? Government? Materials availability? Labor market?
d. Is Production performing to budget? What, if any, areas of variance are there?

4. *Adequate production control reports.* The Production function requires meaningful control reports, issued regularly and with sufficient frequency to permit timely remedial actions. Each report should compare actual to target performance, as well as facilitate the early identification of trends. Are the following measured regularly and effectively:

a. Output to budget? Output to new order input? Order backlog?
b. Turnaround time of remakes and repairs?
c. Productivity: Plant-wide? Departmental? Work center?
d. Costs and expenses to budget? In sufficient detail? Are there major differences between actual and budgeted costs?
e. Performance to production schedule?
f. Staffing to staffing budget?

g. Dollar value of merchandise shipped per direct labor employee? Per "total" employee(s)?
h. Scrap and rework to budget? Per unit of good production?
i. Individual utility usage and cost per unit of production activity?
j. Performance to schedule of active projects for which Production is responsible?
k. Output per hour?

The Materials Management Function

The Materials Management function, which incorporates purchasing, inventory control, and production control, is another source of overall weakness for many businesses. It is susceptible to a number of illnesses, such as fragmentation, oversophistication, and a lack of understanding and respect from the production floor.

A very good manufacturing resources planning (MRP) program provides, at a reasonable price, the various strengths required of the Materials Management function. However, an MRP program that rates below excellent generally costs more than it is worth.

Seven keys to a strong Materials Management function are: (1) accurate, up-to-date, and manageable bills of material and route/process sheets, (2) an effective control system, sophisticated only to the point of maximum return on investment in it, (3) a secured place for everything, and everything in its place, (4) dynamic and accurate transaction reporting, (5) understanding and respect from the production floor, (6) performance to a sound, formal strategic plan, and (7) adequate materials management control reports.

1. Accurate, up-to-date, and manageable bills of material and route/process sheets. The entire Materials Management function will be ineffective unless this information is available in accurate, easy-to-use form.

a. Are bills of material and route/process sheets available in accurate, convenient form?

b. Are purchase specifications clearly stated and only as stringent as necessary?

2. *An effective control system, sophisticated only to the point of maximum return on investment in it.* Many materials management control systems have been disintegrated by well-intentioned, informal minor improvements. Others, on the other hand, are sophisticated to the point of suffocating production performance.

a. Is the system diagrammed and/or described in writing?

b. Has an MRP program been implemented? To what degree? How well does it work? Is it respected by Production?

c. Are cost-effective order quantities established and followed?

d. Is the product/parts numbering system easily administered? Sufficient? Cumbersome to any function that must use it?

e. Does Purchasing have at least two available vendors for each type of material purchased?

f. Are material receipts properly verified, or are they merely copied from shipping papers?

g. Does the Purchasing function shop for and negotiate quality, price, terms, and delivery—or does it merely buy?

h. What is the degree of purchasing expertise in the market areas from which major purchases are made?

i. Where advantageous, are blanket orders used and carefully administered?

j. Is there a formal value analysis program? Is it effective?

k. Are shop loading parameters simple and effective?

l. Have targeted stock-out levels been established

statistically? Are they adequately controlled? What are the actual stock-out levels?

m. Are causes of abnormal stock-outs identified and corrected?

n. How accurate are the forecasts used for materials management scheduling?

o. Are causes of production bottlenecks regularly defined and eliminated?

p. To what degree is one production schedule completed before the next is started?

q. How does Materials Management influence delivery integrity?

r. What is the ratio of "unexpedites" to expedites?

s. What is the level of vendor lock-ins?

t. If there is subcontracted work, how effective is it? Should there be more? Or less?

3. *A secured place for everything, and everything in its place.* Lost material, as well as all time spent in searching for it or in replacing it, is lost money.

a. Is security adequate in each stocking area? Has the responsibility for security been clearly designated?

b. Are there specified staging areas? Do they improve work flow? Has responsibility for each staging area been clearly assigned?

c. Have specific, readily understood addresses been assigned to all storage and staging areas?

d. How much time is spent in searching and expediting? In plant? In purchasing?

4. *Dynamic and accurate transaction reporting.* The closer a business is to accurate, on-line transaction reporting, the more immediate can be its corrective reaction to production problems, and the lower will be its cost of interruptive inquiries on the status of orders.

a. Is the elapsed time between shop transactions and the reporting of them to concerned personnel sufficiently short and cost-effective?

b. Are there adequate in-shop "toll gate" check-points on order status?
c. Are scrap collection, disposal, and reporting aggressive and adequate?
d. What is the level of material handling damages?
e. Is there regularly scheduled cycle counting of inventories? Is it comprehensive? What are the results of actual versus book? Is the system cost-effective?

5. *Understanding and respect from the production floor.* There is little chance that Materials Management can be effective without the wholehearted support of the Production function.

a. Do shop personnel have sufficient understanding of, and commitment to, the materials management system?
b. Are communications between Production and Materials Management of a constructive, positive nature?

6. *Performance to a sound, formal strategic plan.*

a. Are current systems readily expandable to accommodate planned growth?
b. Are sources of planned new materials being developed?

7. *Adequate materials management control reports.* Are the following reported regularly and effectively:

a. Production to schedule?
b. Delivery integrity?
c. Stock-out levels? Trends?
d. Approved vendor lists?
e. Monthly report of savings generated by Materials Management?
f. Monthly report of unit price increases of purchased items?
g. Regular, careful audit of transactions with company(s) that buys your scrap?

h. Purchases delivery due date report?
i. Master schedule?

The Manufacturing/Process Engineering Function

Manufacturing or Process Engineering must be a leading force in cost reduction. A strong function will: (1) save at least five times its cost each year, (2) be well respected by the Production function, (3) perform to a sound, formal strategic plan, and (4) have adequate control reports.

1. Annual savings of at least five times the cost of the function. This function, more readily than all others, lends itself to direct measurement of return on investment in it. Manufacturing/Process Engineering should produce a significant return to be considered successful.

a. Is there a formal methods improvement program? Is it effective?
b. Are machine combinations, crew sizing, and conveyorization aggressively attacked?
c. Are methods, processes, and routings both cost- and quality-effective? Are they clearly defined and improved regularly?
d. Are bottlenecks and capacities evaluated, projected, and improved regularly?
e. Are work standards up-to-date and viable?
f. Are there updated product flow diagrams?
g. What is the level of Manufacturing/Process Engineering participation in equipment purchase decisions?
h. What is the level of participation by this function in new-product decisions? Are methods and processes of new-product production considered far enough in advance? Is there time to properly plan ahead for the routings and layout of new products?

2. The respect of the Production function. This is another of the many cases where one function must be understood and appreciated by at least one other function in order to be most effective.

a. What is the level of coordination with Production in resolving manufacturing problems?
b. Is there rapid and constructive response to production emergencies?
c. Does Production comply with specified processes, routings, machine feeds, and speeds? Does Production participate in the establishment of these specifications?

3. *Performance to a sound, formal strategic plan.*

a. Do processes, routings, layout, facilities, and methods that are in place and in planning conform to the company plan?

4. *Adequate manufacturing/process engineering control reports.* Are the following measured regularly and effectively:

a. Return on investment in this function?
b. Performance to time and dollar schedules on projects?
c. Production productivity improvements?

The Quality Assurance Function

Quality Assurance should be a profit producer that is constantly striving to eliminate the need for itself. Solid management of this function will result in annual earnings contributions through increased sales of better-quality products, decreased costs of rejects and returns, and reduced overall cost of quality (the sum of money lost through defective quality, plus the money spent for quality control).

Five items usually associated with a strong Quality Assurance function are: (1) comprehension of the scope of its function, (2) aggressiveness and success in identifying and eliminating the sources of quality problems, (3) clout, (4) performance to a sound, formal strategic plan, and (5) adequate quality assurance control reports.

1. Quality Assurance's comprehension of the scope of its function. Quality Assurance is the exercise of direction and control over the degree of excellence of the company product(s). The function, in itself, adds no value to the product. The most valid indicator of a successful Quality Assurance function is an ever-increasing ratio of earnings gained through improved quality to cost of the Quality Assurance function.

  a. Have all elements of this ratio been defined? In calculating the ratio, does earnings gained through improved quality include everything from scrap and rework costs through sales and service calls to product liability claims and gained and lost customers? Does cost of the Quality Assurance function include all elements of the total cost of quality assurance?
  b. Are the costs of these elements regularly calculated or officially estimated with assistance from Accounting? Is the ratio reported regularly? What have been the trends?
  c. Is the ratio tested regularly, by estimating the effect of an increase or a reduction in the cost of the Quality Assurance function? What action has been taken?
  d. Do quality assurance personnel understand, and are they committed to, their individual roles in achieving this stated overall objective?

2. Aggressiveness and success in identifying and eliminating the sources of quality problems. Quality problems must be logged as they occur, with suspected cause, recommended remedial action, and targeted correction dates. This log should be reviewed daily to ensure effectiveness.

  a. Are specifications written and viable?
  b. Are inspections to specifications, and not to opinions?

c. Are the subjective quality features well, and consistently, interpreted by inspection personnel?

d. Is there a formal program to identify and correct the causes of defects?

e. At what pace do inspectors work? How much of their time is spent in actually inspecting?

f. Is there a sound incoming inspection procedure? Are approved sampling techniques used? What is the degree of integration with engineering specifications and material control systems?

g. Are inspection and testing built into production equipment where viable and the responsibility of Production?

h. What is the level and formality of communications on customer feedback with sales and marketing personnel? Is feedback utilized?

i. Are the involved quality assurance personnel sufficiently familiar with documental requirements of product liability laws?

3. Clout. To be effective, Quality Assurance must have the authority to stop substandard quality in its tracks, shutting down operations until the problem is corrected or the function is overruled by upper-level general management.

a. What is the authority level of inspectors? Is this level acceptable?

b. Are quality offenders sufficiently and consistently disciplined?

c. Does authority to overrule quality assurance personnel rest with the proper organizational levels and functions?

4. Performance to a sound, formal strategic plan.

a. Are quality assurance techniques in use and in planning, in conformance to the company plan?

5. Adequate quality assurance control reports. Although adequate control reporting is a necessity, it should be recognized that this function frequently produces too much paperwork.

a. Are finished products labeled as necessary, with date, serial number, and inspector identification?
b. Is quality performance reported regularly, in sufficiently short intervals, from all critical areas? What have been the levels and trends of scrap/rejects?
c. Is the science of statistics used to the point of maximum return?
d. Is there a customer complaint follow-up log?
e. Is the cost of the function, as well as its contribution, regularly measured to budget? With what results? Trends?
f. What has been the trend in head count of quality assurance personnel, both absolute and relative to activity?

The Finance and Accounting Function

In addition to the basics of accurate and timely reporting, four factors associated with a strong Finance and Accounting function are: (1) commitment to being an aggressive profit enhancement function, (2) success in eliminating financial surprises, (3) performance to a sound, formal strategic plan, and (4) adequate financial and accounting control reports.

1. Commitment to being an aggressive profit enhancement function. The best Finance and Accounting organizations are oriented to improving the future, rather than only reporting the past. They concentrate on sound cash and risk management, on identification of the best opportunities for cost reduction, and on recommendation of profit-improving actions. They aim at reporting financial history only to the degree necessary to meet legal requirements, protect invested funds, provide adequate control of the business, and improve earnings. They are continually alerting managers in other functions to current and anticipated problems.

a. Are finance and accounting personnel motivated to improve earnings?

b. Is available cash rapidly put to the best use?
c. Are all risks soundly evaluated? Are those beyond the self-absorption level insured, with proper protection, and at a competitive cost?
d. Are areas for potential savings identified frequently, with action recommended?
e. Are cost variances aggressively and accurately analyzed, with sound recommendations for corrective action?
f. Do key personnel understand and communicate well with other functions of the business? Do they conduct regular review meetings of financial statements and accounting control reports?
g. Do heads of other functions understand the accountants' language and reports?
h. To what degree does this function participate in pricing and credit decisions?
i. How strong are relationships with banks and other involved financial institutions?
j. Is the work pace satisfactory? Are all the "bean counters" necessary?

2. *Success in eliminating financial surprises.* Such things as unexpected inventory shortages, insufficient accruals, improper amortizations, and unexpected large expenditures can be extremely damaging to a turnaround program.

a. What is the accuracy of the reporting input into Accounting? Reporting output from Accounting? What have been the trends in accuracy?
b. Have physical inventories been sufficiently accurate and frequent? Trends?
c. Are existing accruals sound? Too small? Too large?
d. Are there unamortized expenses? Any for items that are no longer useful?
e. What is the level of open obligations to vendors? Blanket orders? Any overcommitments?
f. Are receivables and payables properly moni-

tored? What has been the trend in receivables? Are reserves adequate? Too high?

g. Is there an accurate and meaningful cost accounting system?
h. Is there adequate control of capital expenditures? How do actual expenses and savings compare to original estimates?
i. Is there an up-to-date, accurate fixed asset ledger?
j. How do recent pricing actions compare to unit cost trends of major commodities used?

3. *Performance to a sound, formal strategic plan.* The Finance and Accounting function should play a key role in monitoring overall performance to the company strategic plan.

a. Is this function on schedule in attainment of planned goals?
b. Are there sound operating and capital budgeting programs? Is there follow-up action on deviations?
c. Is this function providing the information it should to other functions, in order for them to meet their sections of the strategic plan?
d. Does this function have the most effective degree of authority?

4. *Adequate finance and accounting control reports.* It is extremely important that balance sheets, income statements, and control reports on each key business indicator be accurate, be issued regularly and at the most effective intervals, and contain sufficient, but not unnecessary, detail.

List, under comments, information you consider to be either lacking, inaccurate, or superfluous, in current reports.

The Personnel Function

Before getting into the audit of the Personnel function, three points of major significance should be noted in regard to human resources: (1) People are the key resource of any business. The right people, properly motivated, can make mediocre plans and systems succeed. The best plans and systems fail when used by mediocre people. (2) It is cheaper and more time-efficient to hire good people than to train and develop them. (3) It is very difficult to hire, motivate, and retain top-flight personnel in a company that is not financially healthy and growing.

The four factors that are essential to a strong Personnel function are: (1) sound recruiting and hiring practices, (2) a deep-seated commitment to the dignity and welfare of each employee as an individual, (3) performance to a sound, formal strategic plan, and (4) adequate personnel control reports.

1. Sound recruiting and hiring practices. A significant cost savings is achieved when the right personnel is acquired and retained.

- a. Record of the last 10 salaried employees hired? Last 20 hourly employees hired?
- b. Is there a formal human resources planning program? Are backups being developed for each key position? Are future needs being recognized? Who participates?
- c. Are there formal hiring specifications, agreed on in advance by Personnel with two levels of supervision above the open position?
- d. Who makes the hiring decisions?
- e. Is there well-organized, effective preemployment interviewing, especially for key positions?
- f. What has been the batting average in hiring first choices among candidates for recent openings?

2. A deep-seated commitment to the dignity of each employee as an individual. This cardinal requirement covers the provision of everything from a safe place to work, to a motivational environment that encourages all employees to work to their immediate potential, to tools for each employee to expand that potential.

a. Do all areas provide safe, healthy, pleasant working environments? In what condition are lavatories? Lunch areas?

b. What are the levels of tardiness and absenteeism? Trends? Is there proper and consistent discipline?

c. Do all managers respect their subordinates as individuals?

d. Do subordinates know and respect their superiors?

e. What attitudes are reflected in the faces and paces of employees in the various departments? What are strong and weak areas?

f. Are communications effective? Two-way? Regular? Are there many channels? Are employees kept informed, regularly and honestly, about the business?

g. What is the current employee turnover level? What are the real reasons for turnover? What have been the trends?

h. What percentage of openings are filled by newly hired employees rather than by promotion within?

i. How do salary levels of newly hired employees compare to those of senior employees in similar positions?

j. Is there any evidence, documented or otherwise, of discrimination or harassment?

k. What is the prevailing management style? Participative, entrepreneurial, dictatorial? Is it effective?

l. Are most employee problems resolved promptly and satisfactorily? If there are formal grievances, how many have there been recently and what type?

m. Are personnel problems resolved at the lowest effective organizational level?

n. Have supervisors been trained in, and are they practicing, recognition, job understanding, and job enlargement?

o. Are wage, salary, and benefit levels competitive?
p. If applicable, what is the state of union relations? Why? What have been the trends?
q. Is discipline applied consistently company-wide?
r. Is the organizational structure sound? Is departmentalization effective? Is the number of managerial layers effective? What are the spans of control?
s. Are there incentive programs? Are they effective?
t. Is there a formal program that provides career growth opportunities?
u. Are termination practices documented and constructive? Consistent? What has been the recent feedback from individuals who have terminated their employment?
v. Is plant security adequate? What is the degree of certainty?
w. If applicable, what is being done to improve problem areas in the union contract?
x. Are emergency organizations well trained, and emergency activities well defined?

3. *Performance to a sound, formal strategic plan.* Human resources strategies and objectives should be a major element of any strategic business plan.

a. Have all personnel policies and practices been documented?
b. Is the company in compliance with all applicable laws and regulations governing employment, wages, salaries, benefits, safety, health?
c. Has the proper corporate image been projected to the public? Is the company a good corporate citizen?
d. Is the Personnel function on schedule in attainment of planned goals?

4. *Adequate personnel control reports.* Human resources deteriorate and/or become too expensive without adequate control of the Personnel function.

a. Are organization charts up-to-date and accurate?
b. Are there formal, effective job description and evaluation programs?
c. Is there a sound, formal MBO program?
d. Are disciplinary actions properly documented?
e. Are all accidents reported promptly and documented properly?
f. Are there regular, effective reports of absenteeism, tardiness, turnover, safety, lost-time accidents, current pay levels in the local labor market?
g. Is there a regular monthly report of all formal communications (meetings, notices, newsletters, etc.)?
h. Are there up-to-date emergency call lists where needed?

The Management Information Services Function

The tremendous acceleration of knowledge in the field of office electronics is almost enough in itself to make any MIS function look good. For that very reason, this function will merit a tremendous amount of attention in the immediate future. An MIS function that appears to be outstanding, when compared to prior in-house performance, may be losing very valuable ground to the state of the art as practiced by competitors. In addition, there are many investment traps being offered—financially attractive hardware and software that will be obsolete soon after installation.

At least four ingredients are necessary to a strong MIS function: (1) an MIS function that is not self-serving, but that understands and responds to the overall needs of the business, (2) knowledgeable and accurate interpretation of the future of the mushrooming field of business electronics, (3) performance to a sound, formal business plan, and (4) adequate MIS control reports.

1. An MIS function that is not self-serving, but that understands and responds to the overall needs of the busi-

ness. Many MIS people speak a language not readily understood by others in the business world. Many are committed to another business, data transmission and processing, which often tends to seek its own ends at the expense of the firm it is intended to serve. That language barrier and dichotomy of purpose are serious deterrents to a successful MIS function.

a. Is there frequent and clear two-way communication between MIS and heads of other functions? Are MIS personnel adequately user-oriented, actively seeking user input into systems design?
b. Do MIS personnel understand and appreciate the purpose and needs of other functions? How well do they respond to them?
c. What is the level of MIS awareness of data transmission and processing needs in non-office functions? Its response level?
d. What is the MIS attitude toward urgent requests for information? Response time?
e. What percentage of MIS data output is being used? How much is necessary?
f. Do MIS personnel work with others constructively to identify and eliminate causes for bad data input?
g. Are there fewer or more total employees because of MIS?
h. To what degree do heads of other functions understand and respect MIS performance?

2. Knowledgeable and accurate interpretation of the future of the mushrooming field of business electronics.

a. Are existing computers, peripheral equipment, phone systems, copiers, word processors, and so forth, adequate? Compatible with each other, as well as with the advancing state of the art? Are plans for new equipment sound? Reviewed frequently? Do they provide for contingent directions?

b. Is there intelligent open-mindedness toward hardware and software suppliers? No lock-ins to one vendor? Frequent communications with several vendors to keep abreast of developments?

c. Is there a commitment to ongoing education?

d. What is the level of participation of MIS personnel in office layout planning, as advisors on the subject of accommodating future electronic developments?

e. What has been the past performance record of MIS? Is there obsolescence of equipment? What are the actual versus estimated expenditures and return on investments?

3. *Performance to a sound, formal strategic plan.*

a. Is the MIS function on schedule in attaining its plan objectives?

b. Is MIS providing information needed by other functions to achieve their respective shares of the company strategic plan.

c. Are MIS development and implementation priorities set by MIS alone, or do other functions participate?

4. *Adequate MIS control reports.* Are the following reported regularly and accurately:

a. Projects performance to schedule?

b. Overall return on MIS investment?

c. Percentage of data processing reports issued on schedule?

d. Actual versus estimated project costs and savings?

e. Departmental performance to budget?

The critical functions of your business may not be included here. If this is the case, as suggested at the beginning of this chapter, list your several key functions. Then, under each, thoughtfully list as many questions as you can aimed at providing a sound measure of the overall performance of that function.

5
Classify Each Key Employee As "Yes," "No," or "Maybe"

THIS next step requires you to quickly become acquainted with and evaluate all employees who report directly to you and their immediate subordinates as well.

This personal/professional evaluation has a twofold purpose. First, as the executive in charge, you must rapidly make a number of "yes," "no," or "maybe" decisions regarding each key employee in response to your question, "Should this person be a member of the turnaround team?" It is almost certain that some employees will not be qualified for the contribution that their position must be counted on to make in order for the turnaround to be highly successful. It may be that some positions are not required at all.

You soon will be formulating rapid growth plans. It will take only one weak link in a key position to thwart such plans. Thus it is extremely important to identify your weakest links and to make certain that those persons are strong enough to keep your plan on schedule to meet established goals.

Furthermore, any employees deserving a "no" rating will, for the same reasons that earned them that rating, be able to contribute little to your immediate planning needs and may even be counterproductive at this stage. Shortcomings in attitudes or professional skills will weaken the foundation you are just beginning to build. Competent replacements for the "no"-rated personnel will do a better job in performing to plan, if they are on board early enough to participate in the plan's formulation.

Much care must be given to this evaluation. For example, decisions based on past performance under a prior manager are not always valid. Because you are a better manager, most of your subordinates will be upgrading their performance. Also, "no" decisions create traumatic experiences for the recipients, their families, and often for other employees. Your decisions should not be made lightly.

The second purpose of the evaluation is to determine the psychological wants and needs of each key individual. This information will enable you to provide a superior motivational environment for the persons rated "yes" and "maybe." In addition, it will help you to decide whether each key subordinate has the psychological makeup best suited for long-range satisfaction in his or her line of work. You don't want anyone with you for the long haul who got into a position or function that does not offer that individual personal fulfillment. For example, some positions require and reward drive, while others require and reward patience and perfectionism. A patient perfectionist without much drive may be doing well and be temporarily satisfied in a drive-oriented job. However, that person's chances for outstanding success and satisfaction in the long run are slim without a job change.

The functional audit, which you have just completed, will provide some clues concerning personal weaknesses, because functional weaknesses are frequently a reflection of personal shortcomings in those responsible for that function.

The mutual needs inventory, which you are about to undertake, will also provide guidance in evaluating your key personnel. This exercise requires that each of your staff list what he or she needs, but is not receiving, from each other function. Some weak points in key personnel are sure to surface at this time.

"Yes," "No," or "Maybe"

There are a number of criteria that might be used in rating each of your key people. In most cases the following four will be adequate: integrity, job understanding, commitment, and attitude.

1. Integrity. While reviewing your completed functional audits with the head of each function, you can easily identify the buck-passers and excuse-makers. They automatically qualify for the "maybe" zone because this trait can be corrected in most individuals.

Before going further, I would recommend that all "maybe" ratings for people in the Human Resources function be reclassified as "no," rather than as "maybe." Your top personnel people must project a near-perfect example of the ideal personality. Don't gamble with your need for this by accepting "maybe" people on your turn-around team.

Wide gaps in personal credibility usually become apparent early in the game as well and qualify for a "maybe." Many who fall into this group will correct themselves as soon as they are sure you won't tolerate anything less than absolute integrity. Such changes in personality will not go unappreciated. Others, benefiting from these improvements in credibility, will be outspoken in their increased respect for your efforts.

Chronic prevaricators, if you have any, will probably take more time to identify. Once identified, they should be rated "no." Their divisive influence on your organization will outweigh any and all of their positive contributions.

2. Job understanding. Again two points must be considered. Are the employees sufficiently knowledgeable in their profession to contribute what is needed to the overall task ahead? Surely a "yes" answer to this question is the only acceptable one. Yet this question, too, can seldom be answered immediately. Some guidance might come from the functional audit, the individuals' knowledge of the latest developments in their field, and their eagerness for continuing education. But a number of your people will remain in the "maybe" classification until time permits you to categorize them otherwise.

Second, do all employees fully understand how their positions and functions fit into the overall business picture? Many of your staff may need some help here, if only because you are about to reframe the big picture. Thus this is the one area where a "no" rating should not result in immediate disqualification.

3. *Job commitment.* Without commitment, even the best job understanding results in lukewarm performance. For an effective turnaround, *all* key people must be totally committed to the company, your programs, your style, and their professions. Some indications of commitment are willingness to work long hours on urgent projects, appropriate work pace, minimal extraneous conversations, stick-to-itiveness, willingness to question, interest in company communications, and very positive pro-company remarks. A "maybe" vote here must be converted rapidly to either "yes" or "no" because of your critical need for total commitment.

Turnarounds can represent a special case in regard to the subject of personal commitment. Some people naturally commit themselves to everything they do; some only to things they enjoy; some never seem capable of a high degree of commitment. Be careful not to downgrade those of your people in the middle group. They may have had very little motivation in the past to commit themselves to a failing company with weak leadership.

4. *Attitude.* This element is closely related to commitment, but it deserves its own niche because of its prime importance to the success of your turnaround. Attitudes toward the company, other employees, other departments, and customers must be highly positive. Furthermore, your immediate subordinates must reflect your attitude as well. Accept nothing less than the very best in terms of positive attitudes.

One last comment on this topic. Replace any tyrannical supervisors as soon as possible. They will seriously damage your cause, and the odds against converting them are too great.

Behavior Style

A little more information about all key employees will aid you in evaluating them and enhance the ongoing success of your turnaround program. Knowledge of the basic intelligence level and of the psychological wants and needs of an individual can be valuable tools in the motivation of that person. Understanding the behavior style of a person and the behavior pattern best suited to each job will provide worthwhile information required for long-range job satisfaction.

The performance level of highly motivated personnel almost defies the imagination. I have witnessed the achievement of turnaround results above and beyond what anyone involved had believed possible. In each case, the difference between the turnaround actually attained and what was expected to occur could be attributed solely to the high motivation of the turnaround team.

People can rarely be motivated by others for long periods of time. Others may inspire them, but they must motivate themselves. The capacity for self-motivation becomes almost infinite so long as the wants and needs of those involved continue to be satisfied. By knowing a subordinate's basic intelligence level, you can feed that person's wants and needs in a most digestible manner.

Many certified intelligence tests are available. If your key people were not so tested as part of a prehiring screening procedure, I suggest that you use a test that is familiar to either yourself or the head of your Human Resources function.

A variety of systems exist for evaluating behavior style, wants, and needs. The one I prefer to use is an

Figure 6. Employee and job classification sheet.

Group **General Management**

Name & Position	Is job necessary?	Age	Years of service	Direct subordinates	Total supervised	Annual salary	Intelligence	Business skills	Mechanical aptitude	Sales aptitude	Vocabulary	Integrity	Job understanding	Commitment	Attitude	Dominance	Influencing others	Steadiness	Compliance
								Aptitudes					**Yes, No, Maybe**				**Profiles**		
R. Marcoux Gen'l Mgr	Y	51	8	7	690	70	4	4	4	2	4					5/6	4/3	1/2	4/4
W. Reid Marketing Mgr	Y	45	23	6	39	60	4	1	1	4	2	Y	Y	M	Y	4/4	4/4	2/3	2/2
D. Smith Operations Mgr	Y	41	3	7	557	48	2	4	4	4	4	Y	M	Y	M	3/3	4/3	4/4	4/4
J. Wilkerson Engineering Mgr	Y	36	9	6	18	52	4	1	4	4	2	Y	Y	Y	M	6/6	5/4	2/3	3/4
B. Jardine Q A Mgr	Y	54	1	3	18	38	4	3	2	3	3	M	Y	Y	N	2/3	4/5	4/5	2/3
C. Blair Controller	Y	55	33	3	18	44	4	4	3	1	4	Y	M	Y	M	4/5	4/5	2/4	3/4
T. Colburn Personnel Mgr	Y	34	4	7	24	42	4	4	1	4	4	Y	Y	Y	Y	4/4	4/4	3/3	3/2
F. Pompeo MIS Mgr	Y	42	14	3	9	42	3	4	2	3	1	Y	M	Y	M	5/4	5/3	2/2	4/4
P. Holmes Plant Supt	?	55	23	6	536	42	3	3	4	2	2	Y	Y	Y	Y	4/4	3/4	3/3	5/4

Key:
Aptitudes rated on scale of 1 to 4; Profiles rated on scale of 1 to 6. Profiles are: Normal/Under Pressure

Date _____

Dominance: shapes things by overcoming opposition.

Influence: brings others into alliance.

Steadiness: cooperates with others to complete one task at a time.

Compliance: promotes quality without changing existing circumstances.

Wants & Needs	Comments
W: power and authority. N: to give reasons for conclusions; people concerns, patience, humility.	Results-oriented.
W: control the environment. N: genuine sensitivity; willingness to help others.	Inspirational. Won't commit until she senses she has more control over the company.
W: high personal ambitions. N: to appreciate others; delegation of important tasks.	Practitioner. Bull in a china shop. Needs more job understanding and better attitude toward subordinates.
W: power and authority. N: to give reasons for conclusions; people concerns, patience, humility.	Results-oriented. Short talk will commit him.
W: maintain friendships; keep people happy. N: attention to deadlines; initiative to get things done.	Counselor. Replace. Attitude poor.
W: dominance; the unusual. N: warmth; tactful communication; team cooperation.	Creative. Review job with her. Also, a "can't be done" attitude.
W: control the environment. N: genuine sensitivity; willingness to help others.	Inspirational. Check commitment rating in the "yes, no, maybe" column again. Others on staff question his dedication.
W: control the environment. N: genuine sensitivity; willingness to help others.	Inspirational. Must have better idea of job fit and less desire to be top dog.
W: dominance; the unusual. N: warmth; tactful communication; team cooperation.	Creative. Position should report to operations manager.

effective and inexpensive learning system available from
Performax Systems International, Inc., 12755 State
Highway 55, Minneapolis, Minnesota 55441. My expo-
sure to the work of John Cleaver and Arnold Daniels at
Princeton led to my discovery of Performax's Personal
Profile System.

Most of your people will enjoy participating in such
an evaluation. The Performax System provides the fun
of a gimmicky approach as well as a self-development
booklet for each person to keep along with his or her
test results. After reviewing their results with you, many
employees will request a blank booklet for their spouses
in order to compare results and opinions at home and
thus bring the family into the turnaround on a positive,
participative note.

Figure 6 shows how many of the factors frequently
used to evaluate an individual may be reduced to a handy
and useful reference sheet for the turnaround manager.
This classification sheet is divided into several sections,
as follows:

Need for position. This column addresses the question of whether or not the job is really necessary to the
success of the enterprise.

Personal data. This five-column section provides traditional data about each employee:

Age reached in current calendar year.

Years of service attained in current calendar year.

Number of persons directly supervised.

Total number supervised through subordinates.

Annual base salary (in thousands of dollars).

Aptitudes. Preemployment aptitude test scores are
noted on a scale of 1 to 4, with 4 being very high and 1
being very low, for:

Intelligence
Business skills
Mechanical aptitude

Sales aptitude

Vocabulary

"Yes," "no," "maybe" ratings. Here you note your opinion of each individual with regard to:

Integrity

Job understanding and professional ability

Commitment

Attitude

Behavior style. Note personal profile levels on a scale of 1 (lowest) to 6 (highest), both under normal conditions (top figure) and under pressure (bottom figure), measuring:

Dominance

Influence

Steadiness

Compliance

The upper right-hand section suggests how persons with 6, 5, or 4 in the Profile section usually go about getting things done.

Wants and needs. Jot down a few key words relative to the wants (W) and needs (N) of each person in the group. These provide you with a convenient reminder and guide.

Comments. In this column, the first word relates to the individual's classic behavior pattern as described by Performax and provides a quick reference for a deeper look into that person's wants and needs. Other words are comments by you.

Chapter 6 expands on the use of the classification sheet.

6

Take Action
on the Ratings
of Key Employees

NOW that all key employees have been classified, it is time to take action on these classifications.

"Yes"-rated personnel must be motivated to a significant level if the turnaround program is to be a very good one. "No"-rated employees must be separated from the company as soon as possible in order to remove their bottlenecking effect. And, of course, each "maybe" rating must be converted to either a "yes" or a "no," with appropriate follow-up action.

Let's use the cases of several of the employees classified in Figure 6 to show how this might be done.

Motivating the "Yes" Employee

Judd Wilkerson, the engineering manager, has acceptable integrity, job understanding, and commitment. But his attitude was rated "maybe," because Roger Marcoux, the general manager in charge of the turnaround, had heard several comments regarding his failure to cooperate with other members of the staff.

Judd's behavior pattern shows him to be highly results-oriented. The Performax program and others similar to it note that results-oriented individuals tend to have high ego strength and tend to display irritation, independence, impatience, faultfinding, and bluntness.

It is clear to Mr. Marcoux that the questions concerning Judd's attitude are attributable primarily to his results-oriented personality and that results will be needed in the turnaround. It is just as clear to Mr. Marcoux that the feelings of the others toward Judd will be mollified as soon as the staff becomes more exposed to dealing with behavior patterns, and after he has had a short talk with Judd about this pattern of his. He thus rerates Judd as a "yes" on attitude.

The general manager's decision to retain Judd was based in part on his determination that the position of engineering manager is needed in the turnaround, and on Judd's high levels of intelligence, mechanical aptitude, and sales aptitude. He also noted that Judd's vocabulary is limited and he has a very low level of business skills. In the future he will: be on guard against misinterpreting Judd as a result of his poor choice of words, be on the lookout for paperwork errors from him, and be certain that a highly competent secretary types all of his outside letters.

Getting back to Judd's behavior pattern, a good analysis tool would also indicate the following about the results-oriented personality:

Emotions: high ego strength; displays irritation and independence.

Goal: dominance and independence.

Judges others by: ability to accomplish the task quickly.

Influences others by: force of character; persistence.

Value to the organization: "show 'em" attitude.

Overuses: impatience.

Under pressure: becomes critical and fault finding; resists participating in a team; may overstep prerogatives.

Fears: will be taken advantage of by others; slowness; being too jovial.

Would increase effectiveness with more: verbalization of reasons for conclusions; people concerns; patience; humility.

This person's tendencies include: getting immediate results; causing action; accepting challenges, making quick decisions; questioning the status quo; taking authority; causing trouble; solving problems.

This person needs others who: weigh pros and cons; calculate risks; use caution; structure a more predictable environment; research facts; deliberate before deciding; recognize the needs of others.

This person desires an environment that includes: power and authority; prestige and challenge; opportunity for individual accomplishment, wide scope of operations; direct answers; opportunity for advancement; freedom from controls and supervision; many new and varied activities.

To be more effective, this person needs: difficult assignments; understanding that he/she needs people; techniques based on practical experience; an occasional shock; identification with a group; to verbalize the reasons for conclusions; an awareness of existing sanctions; to pace self and relax more.

Mr. Marcoux decides to call Judd into his office, discuss his behavior pattern with him, and assign him the task of putting together a product offerings proposal for the upcoming strategic planning session. He will probably point out the importance of this project, mention the tight time schedule of 30 days, and stress the significance of the input Judd is to seek from Marketing, Manufacturing, and Accounting. (He makes a note to explain this assignment in advance to Wendy Reid, the marketing manager, who will have her own schedule for preparing a comprehensive study of markets and competition during that same period.)

All of the "yes"-rated personnel may be handled in a fashion similar to that used by Mr. Marcoux with Judd.

Again, a word of caution. Aptitude weaknesses and poor personality fits between person and job usually show up in the ratings of integrity, commitment, and/or attitude. However, this is not always the case. Occasionally, individuals with four "yes" ratings lack an aptitude that you, the turnaround executive, deem necessary or may have an element of personality that you do not appreciate. Such a shortcoming would be cause for separation, if you believe it to be sufficiently serious.

Finally, you must continue to motivate your staff regularly through personal recognition and job enlargement and by servicing their individual wants and needs.

Separating the "No" Employee

The "no"-rated employee should be separated (and replaced, if the position is necessary to the turnaround) as soon as possible.

For this example, let's look at Bob Jardine, the quality assurance manager in Figure 6.

The general manager notes that Bob has a low mechanical aptitude, a shortcoming he would prefer not to have in that position. He recalls having rated Bob as a "maybe" on integrity for two reasons. Product integrity was suspect and Bob was responsible for product quality. Also, a number of times Bob had blamed customer quality complaints on the Production and Engineering departments. This consideration generated a "no" rating on attitude.

Bob's behavior pattern indicates that he tends to be ambivalent under pressure, to lack initiative, to miss deadlines, to be overly tolerant of nonproducers, and to go out of his way to maintain friendships. Mr. Marcoux decides that: (1) Bob does exhibit these traits, (2) they are not what he desires in his quality assurance manager, (3) other turnaround problems merit a higher priority than does an attempt to change Bob's character, and therefore (4) Bob must be replaced.

Decisions on the "no"-rated personnel in any turnaround situation may be reached in a manner similar to that just described.

Once the termination decision has been made, immediate action must be taken. Such decisions have an uncanny way of leaking out to people who should have no advance knowledge of them. Furthermore, many executives have trouble biting the separation bullet and lose some of their effectiveness while worrying over a separation decision on which they have not acted. For the sake of the turnaround executive, the organization, and the person to be terminated, action must be swift.

In cases where there is sufficient tangible evidence to warrant separation, the employee involved should be terminated immediately. The termination interview should be conducted by the turnaround executive, and the reasons honestly explained to the individual being terminated. If the company's termination pay policy is conservative, something more than the normal severance pay should be granted, to compensate for the short time period during which the individual was judged.

In cases where the evidence is sketchy, you might quickly establish some specific short-range objectives for the person in question. Failure to meet these critical objectives in the urgency of a turnaround could then become the basis for separation. If the employee meets the objectives, however, he will have demonstrated that he does deserve further consideration by you.

Bob Jardine, for example, might be given two weeks to a month to accomplish two specific quality improvement projects. If he fails to complete them satisfactorily and on time or if the manner in which he completes them is unsatisfactory, just cause for separation will have been provided. On the other hand, if Bob Jardine does successfully complete the projects, the turnaround manager should continue to assign objectives to him and should closely evaluate his progress in meeting them.

If the vacated position is considered necessary to the turnaround, a replacement must be found and installed in the position as soon as possible.

Deciding on the "Maybe" Employee

After performing much the same exercises as those described for each immediate subordinate, you may still find one or two in the "maybe" category. These must be reclassified as "yes" or "no" in very short order, so that turnaround time is not sacrificed, nor its success diluted.

A second review of aptitude levels and behavior characteristics will aid you in reaching a decision. But the most important tool will be a second interview— your personal contact with the individuals in question. For such a meeting, you should be pre-armed with the behavior pattern data and with some test questions aimed at gaining more information on the employee's integrity, job understanding, commitment, and attitude, which will further crystallize your opinions. Some interviews may require a hard statement of what will and will not be tolerated, followed by a 30-day observation period to determine whether there has been a satisfactory change in performance. Occasionally, you may not be certain whether an employee fully understands the nature of his job. In such cases you may have to resort to assigning a short project or to obtaining the opinion of a professional in the field (this professional could be either someone available at corporate headquarters or an outside associate of yours), to come in and judge whether a key employee has the job knowledge necessary to adequately support the turnaround program.

Now that you have your turnaround team together,

it is time to erase all suspicions and negative thoughts that you may still have concerning the members. You know their strengths; exploit them. You know their weaknesses; buttress them or avoid them. You know their personalities; motivate them. It is important to think of their weaknesses in the human "we all have them" sense, rather than in the negative.

This is the team you have decided to fly with. Use your positive support to keep them enjoying their flight to success.

7

Establish Sound Working Relationships with Key Outside Contacts

UP to this point in the process of determining where the organization stands at present, the entire focus has been internal. It is time now to establish personal contacts with key outsiders who are close to your organization. These usually include executives of major customers and suppliers, but may also involve representatives from your bank, government agencies, the chamber of commerce, and so forth.

Select those who do, or should, have an interest or stake in your company. If possible, meet them by appointment at their places of business. Until you know these people better, it is best not to inconvenience them in any way, nor to entertain them. Be wary in making exceptions to this point, especially if your firm is in debt to them and/or they are aware of your need for a turnaround. Even if a member of your staff advises: "The best way to get to Mr. Doe is to wine and dine him," you may find that that may be the best approach for your staff member but not the best one for you—or your company, in view of its current situation. Visit these outside contacts at their offices; entertainment and dog and pony shows may have their place later in the turnaround program.

You have waited until now to make these contacts

in order to have prepared yourself with a sound grasp of your business, attained as outlined in earlier chapters of this book. Under certain circumstances, you may not be able to wait this long for these visits. This is especially true in cases of critical obligations. Representatives of banks or vendors to whom you are in financial arrears, dissatisfied customers with large axes to grind, and others may be on your doorstep soon after you arrive on the job, to "see what you are going to do about it." If they get to you first, you will be in a negative position of having to react to them and, perhaps, of having to put them off until you have had time to properly answer their inquiry. If at all possible, contact such persons before they contact you, placing yourself in an action position and placing them in the reaction mode. Get all the leverage you can by maneuvering yourself into positions of quiet strength.

Contacts with key outside executives serve several purposes. First, as mentioned earlier, the people you contact are those who do, or should, have a selfish interest in the success of your company. These personal contacts will provide you with a forum for revitalizing that interest where it may have waned, as well as for convincing others that you are the person who, as head of your organization, can best serve their interests in it. The latter is of particular value in instances where the contact has been directly involved in transactions in which your company has failed to perform satisfactorily.

The task of impressing a banker who extended you a loan that you have been delinquent in repaying, or a customer who has been disturbed by your product quality or your delivery performance, or a supplier to whom your payments have been in arrears is not an easy one. It will be even more difficult if you are following several predecessors who failed in a turnaround attempt or if you have been in your position for some time. Very careful planning is required to get these people to believe, or at least to have high hopes, that you are more proficient than your predecessor(s). And you must leave these people with the feeling that you can make the turnaround, and that they will benefit from it.

Second, these contacts should provide you with valuable outside perceptions of your firm, which you probably were not able to obtain from those on the inside. Valid or not, these perceptions have meaning to those who advance them, and thus have merit, because they influence their attitudes and actions.

If your contacts are typical of most groups, they will have a number of misconceptions, both positive and negative, about your company. Your meetings with them present an opportunity for you to immediately correct negative misconceptions. Their comments about areas in which they believe the company is better than it really is should either be filed mentally for consideration in your future planning or corrected immediately.

On the other hand, factual negative perceptions should be remedied on your return to your place of business or should become part of future planning. Factual positive perceptions should be exploited in your future programs.

Be prepared for statements that reflect a complete misunderstanding of your organization, resulting from someone in it having overplayed his or her role with your contact. "We think the world of George. He is doing an outstanding job in heading your Finance Department." George is the credit manager you have already decided to replace.

Third, you are going to need cooperation from these contacts. Enlist it. Approach the subject as if your purpose were to establish a long-term business relationship. However, be careful not to create either specific long-term commitments or personal ties that will result in their bypassing your organization and contacting you directly every time they need service.

The following approaches usually contribute to

achieving the three stated purposes for establishing such working relationships:

1. Approach all contacts with the respectful assumption that they know their business.
2. Do your homework before each meeting. Obtain adequate knowledge of the person you are about to see, of the organization that person represents, and of your company's relationship with both.
3. Don't promise anything that you are not absolutely sure you can deliver.
4. Ask many questions. Avoid the impression that you are telling the contacts to do anything.
5. Show a sincere interest in their businesses. There may be a number of things you don't know about their services or products that could be of benefit to your business.
6. Don't criticize your predecessors, subordinates, or competitors, nor those of your contacts.
7. Don't attempt to be lavish in what you say or do.
8. Take notes in a small looseleaf notebook, making certain to have removed any previously used pages before the meeting. This is to create the impression that your contact stands alone and is far from being buried with your other notes.
9. Maintain an arm's-length relationship, no matter what temptations might be offered to you to come closer.
10. Within two days after each meeting, send your contacts a short note of thanks, including, if possible, a conservative compliment about their organizations and a comment on action you have already initiated to benefit their firms.

The remainder of this chapter is devoted to suggestions that apply specifically to the three groups of outside executives most frequently contacted at this stage in a turnaround program, those representing customers, suppliers, and financial institutions.

Customers

For purposes of this section, companies may be classified in one of two categories: those that sell directly to
a mass market and those that do not. If your firm is in
the former group, you should not contact your present
and potential customers at this time. Wait until you know
where you are going and how you intend to get there.
Only after you have decided exactly what you plan to
sell, and how you plan to sell it, will it be of any great
value to contact your customers through your usual
channels of the media, mail, and so forth. Also, because
of the breadth of the marketplace, the time required to
obtain a representative market sample through personal visits negates that approach. In some instances,
there is a case for utilizing a consulting firm to survey
mass market wants and opinions. However, third-party
surveys tend to be fraught with pitfalls. If used, exercise
extreme care both in selecting a consultant and in accepting all the consultant's conclusions at face value.

For companies in the second group, where a visit
with a dozen or fewer key customers represents an adequate sampling of the market, preliminary contacts at
this time are generally very worthwhile.

Visit customers before visiting vendors and financial institutions, except in circumstances where urgent
credit problems or the need for capital funds dictate a
reversal in sequence. It is the customers who are the
group most necessary to the turnaround. They are the
everyday source of cash and are the most difficult to retain or replace. Your banker, if aware of your need for a
turnaround, will be impressed that you have already
made personal contact with a representative number of
customers, as well as by the specific items of good news
you relay from those meetings. Your suppliers will be
similarly influenced. Both your banker and your suppliers know that your customers are the source of the
funds they receive from you.

If you plan and execute your customer visits properly, you will probably uncover several major business opportunities as a result of them. Not uncommon are the following two examples, drawn from actual preturnaround customer visits.

The first example involves a general manager, new to her position in a company that sold primarily to midwestern original equipment manufacturer (OEM) accounts. During a swing through this market, the general manager was appalled when her customers, with only one exception, complained vociferously about her company's poor delivery performance. She knew that her company records showed that better than 90 percent of all orders were delivered complete and on time. Realizing that something was amiss, the general manager asked to see the customers' copies of their purchase orders. On comparing these with copies she had with her of orders received at her factory, she noticed that in almost every case, the delivery date on her copies was later than that shown on the customers' documents. The general manager immediately identified the cause of the discrepancy as a bad order-entry practice on the part of her sales personnel. In this case, customers traditionally submitted their orders to sales representatives, who rewrote them for the factory. But the rewrites took place after phone calls from the salespeople to friends in production supervision at both factories (theirs and the customers') to determine "when the customer really needed the products that were ordered," and "when the salespeople's company could reasonably expect to produce them." The requested delivery dates, as the salespeople then wrote them, were thus a compromise based on these two inputs. To further complicate the situation, order acknowledgments were all mailed to the salespeople who then failed to deliver them to their customers. The general manager promised immediate correction of the problem and achieved it in her hotel room that evening, merely by dictating a directive to her secretary, which instituted direct company-to-company flow of orders and acknowledgments. She revisited those same customers within 60 days. The customers were sufficiently impressed with the improved delivery performance that the general manager was able to sell them on accepting a 33 percent price increase, saving her business, which otherwise would have failed. While this example may sound as if it could have happened only in small seat-of-the-pants businesses, all companies involved were large divisions of major industrial organizations.

The second example occurred during a new general manager's initial visit to a large manufacturer that was purchasing about half of its needs for one product line from his company. During the visit, it was discovered that the customer used a far greater quantity of another product line from another company—and this product line was the most profitable of any sold by the general manager's company. Furthermore, the competitions' product and delivery were considerably inferior. "I didn't know you people made that," remarked the customer when this was brought to his attention. The general manager accepted a large order on the spot, which eventually led to a threefold increase in his company's sales and a sixfold increase in profits from this one major customer. However, it took some time for this general manager's head to stop shaking, as he recalled the many recorded visits of his sales and technical personnel to that customer over the recent years.

These examples, rather than representing isolated cases, are typical of some of the basic mistakes that lead to the need for business turnarounds. Many can be corrected by just such simple means as these preliminary customer visits.

When visiting customers, it usually pays to take a ranking member of your Sales and Marketing organization with you, as well as the particular sales representative for each account. This will provide answers you might otherwise not be able to provide and enhance the customers' perception of the close personal support you give your Sales and Marketing organization. It will also provide a learning experience for your sales personnel, as they observe your techniques and style.

It is important to do some homework before each visit. Learn the volume and type of business obtained from the customer in question, the customer's strengths and weaknesses, and the details of any recent problems you have had with each other. Also, take copies of any open orders with you.

The most successful approach in conducting each customer visit is to project a sincere image of each customer's importance to your firm, of your wanting to help the customer, and of your delivery integrity. One means of creating this image is to start, after the introductory amenities have concluded, with a statement of your purpose: "I wanted to meet you, to thank you for your business, and to see whether there is anything I can do to help you." Then, let the customer talk, while you actively listen, taking notes on cogent points the customer raises.

The value of this "How can I help you?" approach cannot be overemphasized. It has helped significantly in a number of turnarounds. For example, a newly appointed president of a company in need of a turnaround tried it on the first of a number of wholesaler customers she was visiting. The wholesaler immediately responded, "You're the first executive from one of our suppliers to come here and sincerely ask that question. All of the others spent their entire time extolling their products and services and telling us how to sell more of them." This prompted the president to quickly launch a "How may I help you?" customer-visits campaign. As a result, she soon doubled her business in the large metropolitan area served by her company.

During the early stages of your meeting, try to keep the customer talking. When conversation lags, ask a question or insert a simple active listening statement, such as, "That must have been profitable for you," "You must have been angered by that," "I suppose that was a major disappointment for you," and so forth. Such seemingly innocuous remarks are very effective in gaining the respect of others, in keeping them talking, and in bringing out meaty information. Managers proficient in this technique can gain respect for their intelligence and their concern for another during a first meeting, without ever having said anything of substance about business.

A general manager was supplying about 20 percent of the requirements of a particular customer. Two competitors' companies were supplying the other 80 percent. While visiting this customer, the general manager tried this technique. By utilizing an active listening approach, he gained the respect of his customer and, after some time, finally drew out the fact that his product was preferred, except for a packaging flaw that was strongly objected to by the customer's materials handlers. The customer went so far as to recommend a specific packaging improvement, which had been suggested to her by someone in her receiving warehouse. Upon checking, the general manager found that the suggested package was less expensive than the one his company had been using and superior to those used by his competitors. The package was changed within a week, and the company rapidly gained sales penetration, including a 60 percent share of the visited company's business.

Whatever you do during these customer visits, don't attempt to monopolize or control the meetings, and don't fill in the low spots by trying to impress customers or by telling them what they should do.

Industrial concerns in need of a turnaround almost always have problems with their delivery integrity. They fail in at least one phase of their obligation to deliver what the customer expects in quality, service, and service life, in the period of time that the customer expects to receive it. This problem is relatively easy to resolve with disciplined cooperation among internal departments and disciplined production control. That delivery integrity is a way of life for most successful companies attests to this fact. If your company has this problem, assure the customer that it will be corrected within 30 days. Then correct it by implementing the necessary controls in that time frame.

In the course of each meeting, you will find opportune times to utilize your homework. Without overdoing it, compliment the customer on specific strengths. If past problems existed with an account, mention the steps taken to remedy them at your end and draw out suggestions from the customer concerning what might be done to improve things at the customer's end.

Again, if properly conducted, these initial customer visits will pay for themselves many times over, in both immediate and long-range returns.

Bankers

Contacts with bankers fall into two categories—either courtesy calls or sales calls. If the company in need of a turnaround is a division of a larger concern, financial relations are most often handled by corporate headquarters. In such cases, the company in question may have little more than local checking accounts to cover payroll and day-to-day operating expenses. Here the bank visit need be no more than a courtesy call to an appropriate official of the respective branch bank(s), for the purpose of meeting each other. It is best not to divulge any more than the most general information about the business during such a meeting.

An intermediate situation occurs when you have responsibility for finance but have no immediate problems regarding borrowed funds. In this case, an approach similar to that used in customer visits is quite effective. You probably will be contacting a higher-ranking officer of the bank than for the courtesy call just discussed—the officer directly responsible for financial relations with your company. As such, that officer will be familiar with your financial history. You might also expect her to believe, at least to some degree, that a company cannot be successful unless its chief executive is capable in the fields of finance and accounting. Therefore, be prepared to communicate some of your knowledge of these areas during your initial get-together. This applies especially if you anticipate a future need for funds or an extension of credit.

Take your in-house financial representative with you on all these bank visits. This can fortify your image of interest in financial matters and might facilitate the answering of some questions raised at the meeting.

If you are responsible for finance and have urgent financial problems, considerably more preparation will be required before you meet with representatives of your bank or lending institution. In this circumstance, your task is to sell your company and yourself as a good risk for additional funds or an extension of credit. (A discussion of the advantages and disadvantages of alternative sources of capital funds is beyond the scope of this book.)

The basic purpose of your first meeting will vary with the urgency of the situation. If you don't need financial help at once, this first encounter with your banker will be for informational purposes. In other words, the meeting will give you an opportunity to size up the banker, to determine which approach might work best when you return at a later date to request additional financial support.

If you can delay asking for such added support at this first meeting, this is by far the best route to take. When you do ask for funds, not only will you have already developed some knowledge and understanding of the person(s) representing your source for capital funds but, more important, you will have a well-thought-out strategic plan to support your request. A well-constructed, well-presented, strategic plan works like a skeleton key in opening bank vaults to your needs. More about this in Chapter 13.

In order to best accomplish the objectives of this initial encounter, several items merit careful consideration in your preparation, as well as at the actual meeting. You and the financial subordinate who accompanies you must convey absolute unanimity in your confidence that a turnaround can and will be made and in any preliminary thoughts you advance about turnaround plans. For this reason, some chief executives rightfully prefer to attend these meetings alone.

Next, you must project a strong grasp of your company's financial data, as well as your ability to correctly interpret it. It is usually important that you, rather than your financial subordinate, take the lead in presenting this information. Executives of financial institutions seem to respond more favorably when they perceive that you are directing all phases of your business and that you are knowledgeable about each one of them.

You can reinforce this last point by relating a recent accomplishment or a program that you have implemented in each of several functions of your organization. Just recently, a top officer of a large bank was criticizing a president who had just been terminated for his failure to turn around a company in which the bank had a sizable investment. "I should have known he wasn't the man for the job," he told me, "when all he kept talking about was his Sales and Marketing function."

Also, if at all practical, include in your conversation a few of the specific improvements resulting from your recent visits with customers.

In discussing those meetings with customers, a "How can I help you?" approach was suggested. However, in meetings with bankers, it is recommended that while still being receptive to their suggestions, you convey an "I can do it" image.

Suppliers

One of the primary considerations in meeting with suppliers is whether or not they also sell to your competitors. Vendors are frequently the communications grapevine for entire industries represented by their customers. Many believe, rightly or wrongly, that divulging information about a competitor of a customer to that customer will aid them in making a sale. Therefore, while talking with your suppliers, gather as much information as you can about your competitors without divulging anything that might be used to advantage by them.

If your company has no critical problems with its major vendors, no problems that might deter a turnaround, it is best not to take the time to visit them now. Advise your purchasing manager to introduce your suppliers' sales representatives to you during their regular visits. At some later date, arrange to visit the premises of those few suppliers, if any, on which you are significantly dependent.

Many companies in need of a turnaround do have urgent vendor problems, especially in good economic times, when the vendor has sufficient business from other accounts. Ailing companies, because of delinquent payments or for other credit-related reasons, are given lowest-priority consideration by their suppliers, which often amounts to no consideration at all. The materials they order are delivered too late, or they are forced to pay a premium price or to accept inferior quality.

Such a situation is of major consequence to the firm in need of a turnaround. An immediate meeting with vendors in this category is mandatory.

A satisfactory solution can be devised in almost all circumstances if such meetings are handled properly. In that the solution is often a compromise, be prepared by knowing the limits to which you can extend your organization. This is of even greater importance after an agreement has been reached, because a single failure to meet the accepted future payment plan could interrupt the flow of materials necessary to the success of your turnaround program.

Have those of your staff who can best serve the particular needs of the situation accompany you to each of these meetings.

The tone of your meetings with vendors depends largely on the circumstances and individual personalities involved. Thus, your meetings with vendors tend to vary much more in style than do your meetings with customers or bankers. Your ability to convey that you have a sincere desire to remedy the current problem, the talents needed to do this, and a specific payback plan will guide your meetings with vendors along a common track and enhance your bargaining position.

As mentioned earlier, it is better to be in the position of action than of reaction. Also, after the present problem has been summarized, many suppliers will ask, "What do you propose?" For these two reasons, make your specific proposal for returning to good credit terms before the vendors make theirs. The vast majority of vendors will be extremely receptive and want to work with you.

I am aware of two new chief operating executives in very different turnaround situations who were told by their staffs that preferred suppliers would no longer sell to them because of severe payment delinquencies. In both cases, a visit to each supplier, with a specific, but very conservative, payback proposal opened the gates at once for the resumed flow of materials and services.

If suppliers believe you are sincere, and if they see a mutually beneficial arrangement commencing in the near future, they will want to work with you. Thus it is sometimes advisable to go beyond the present credit problem, stressing such items as the additional business the suppliers may receive from your turned-around company, to cement the concept of mutual benefit.

Generally, the best tone for success at such encounters is one that falls between that suggested for customers and that suggested for bankers. Until a satisfactory agreement is reached, you should remain flexible in steering your course between "How can I help you?" and "How I can help you."

Others

Depending on the circumstances, contacts with key personnel of other outside organizations may be called for at this time. Government agencies, elected officials, landlords, and community services are typical of this group.

Guidelines for meetings with these people are much the same as those set forth above. If either urgency or courtesy dictates the need for such a meeting, undertake it at this time; prepare for it; establish objectives and a tentative plan for attaining them. If such dictates do not apply, postpone getting together until after the strategic plan is developed.

One last point is in order regarding corporate citizenship meetings. If the turnaround organization is located in a smaller city or town where the community has a visible stake in the success of that business, immediate contact with the local chamber of commerce or leading community service organization is strongly recommended.

Note that this chapter applies, as do all others, not just to whole-company turnarounds but also to turnarounds that are restricted to a beleaguered department or a portion of a company. In the latter case, other departments that benefit most from the services of the segment in question might be considered as customers, the accounting department as bankers, and departments serving the turnaround section as suppliers.

8
Solicit Opportunities from Key Personnel

THIS chapter covers the final steps in assessing the current status of the organization to be turned around. By now all key personnel have been advised of the basic objective and have been involved at the fringes of the financial inventory, functional audit, key personnel evaluations, and visits with major outside contacts. If the correct turnaround team was selected, each member, consciously or unconsciously, has been developing a personal list of the most urgent problems to be attacked and the most rewarding opportunities to be realized.

The team members probably have already discussed some of their ideas among themselves. A number of their thoughts may still be in rudimentary stages, but many will have been honed and polished to a reasonable level of soundness.

Now is the time to formally solicit their suggestions. Two formats are recommended for taking this important step: an internal needs list and a tabulation of corporate problems and opportunities.

After these two exercises have been completed, all the assessments made thus far will be summarized in a form conducive to use in future short- and long-range planning.

The Internal Needs List

The head of each business function prepares an internal needs list. This list describes what that function needs but is not now receiving from each other function in order to perform as effectively as possible. A second list includes items now received but not needed. The purpose of the second list is to free up some time for supplying the needs on the first list. The purposes of both are to add a new internal dimension to the turnaround assessment, to stimulate beneficial discussion, and to foster improved teamwork.

You can best inaugurate this element of the program at a staff meeting chaired by you and attended by the head of each function for which an internal needs list will be prepared.

Open the meeting with a brief summary of the "where we stand now" analyses completed thus far, highlighting the more salient points brought out by each evaluation. State further that the assessment phase of the turnaround program is rapidly winding to a close and will soon be followed by the establishment of specific short- and long-range objectives. Close the preliminaries of the meeting by emphasizing that the roles of staff members are becoming considerably more active, beginning now!

In getting into the purpose for the session at hand, announce that the subject is not only a critical step in the turnaround process but a worthwhile educational experience and a challenge to the staff's ability to work together as a team. Members of the staff will be given a chance to see just how professionally they can make and take constructive criticism.

To date, many ideas have been advanced concerning what the organization might best do to increase its return on assets employed, both by building up its income and by reducing its costs. The staff is now going to be asked to view that picture from a completely different perspective. Each staff member is to furnish a list of items needed by that person's function to make it more effective. The lists are to be limited to items that could be furnished by other functions within the business but that at present are not being regularly received.

Indicate that a second, subordinate list will also be required of items that are now received from other functions but that are considered unnecessary or of questionable value when compared to the costs of providing them.

Many of the items on both lists can be expected to relate to informational needs, but physical factors such as improved product quality must also be considered.

Quickly identify the functions to be included in this survey, and request the completed lists from the functional heads within one week. Point out that the lists should include, as specifically as possible, each item needed, a statement of why it is considered necessary, and an estimate of its annual dollar value.

Blank internal needs list forms should then be distributed at the meeting. Sample forms, with examples of items that might be listed, are shown in Figure 7.

Then point out to members of the staff that this assignment serves several other useful purposes:

1. It expresses truly mutual needs. All staff members usually benefit from the satisfaction of each other's valid functional needs, in that they are all together in the company boat. In addition, many individual needs are interrelated. The examples in Figure 7 show how three separate needs must be satisfied if the company is to deliver on time and thus produce at least an additional $152,000 in annual pretax earnings.

It would be in order at this point to refer to one of the basic precepts of management as it relates to these lists: Good management always results in making the whole exceed the sum of its parts. The results achieved by people working well together will be greater than those that would be achieved by the same people work-

Figure 7. Internal needs lists.

By _____		Date _____
		Page ____ of ____
	Internal Needs List	
Needed by ___Manufacturing___	Needed from ___Engineering___	

Item	Why Needed	Estimated Pretax Annual Value
1. Accurate, up-to-date bills of material.	1. Reduce inventory. Fewer parts shortages. Maintain delivery schedules.	$200,000

The Manufacturing function's list of what it needs, but is not receiving, from the Engineering function.

By _____		Date _____
		Page ____ of ____
	Internal Needs List	
Needed by ___Manufacturing___	Needed from ___Marketing___	

Item	Why Needed	Estimated Pretax Annual Value
1. 3-month sales forecasts to ±5%. 3- to 6-month forecasts to ±10%.	1. Reduce inventory. Lower material costs. On-time deliveries. Improved resource.	$50,000

The Manufacturing function's list of what it needs, but is not receiving, from the Marketing function.

By _____		Date _____
		Page ____ of ____
	Internal Needs List	
Needed by ___Marketing___	Needed from ___Manufacturing___	

Item	Why Needed	Estimated Pretax Annual Value
1. 95% complete and on-time deliveries.	1. Sales penetration will improve by 20%.	$152,000

The Marketing function's list of what it needs, but is not receiving, from the Manufacturing function.

ing alone toward the same goal. Because of this phenomenon, it is the general rule that estimated earnings gains, as expressed in the needs lists, will be conservative. Don't spend time justifying these estimates, time that can be better spent in the management effort required to exceed them.

2. It compels the head of each function to think of things needed to perform that function more effectively. Typical functional managers tend to tunnel their thinking to areas in which other functions might improve their performances. Most businesses could be improved significantly if all their managers diverted the time spent in analyzing and criticizing other functions to analyzing and improving their own.

3. As managers make note of what they require from other functions so that their functions can perform more effectively, they will begin to realize that they are not on a one-way street. Others will be listing what they need from them. Such thinking will nourish the seeds of teamwork and cooperation.

4. These lists will bring forth some corporate needs not yet considered that will benefit the turnaround program. Corporate needs uncovered in this way usually require a little time and effort to transform into profit, but such time and effort will be well invested.

5. The heads of the functions will also be forced to review their overall responsibilities while preparing their needs lists. Such reviews frequently uncover some prime opportunities for earnings enhancement that had been overlooked—opportunities within the preparers' own functional areas.

Note the case of a marketing vice president who had shied away from advertising, delegating it completely to a subordinate, who managed an effective program, well within budget. While thinking of his advertising responsibility in preparing his needs list, this executive thought of a simple method for saving $50,000 a year in advertising, without diminishing its effectiveness.

6. In having to quantify their needs, staff members

must consider the costs and financial opportunities in various segments of their functions. Such refreshment of awareness is of value in itself and will prepare these key personnel for the all-important step of quantifying various alternatives to be considered in future short- and long-range plans.

7. Discussion of each other's needs lists at a follow-up staff meeting will, in addition to promoting the team concept, provide each head with an awareness of the responsibilities and concerns of the others. All will see how the others view their own functions, as well as how they view the integrated corporate whole.

8. The lists and follow-up meeting will provide you with a better grasp of the professionalism, creativity, depth of thought, and breadth of understanding of the subordinates involved.

After describing the internal needs project and touching on its values, you should open the meeting to staff input and discussion. At this time, offer a few obvious suggestions for needs that might be listed, such as the needs noted in Figure 7 or the need for some regular reports not currently being issued. You may even want to offer to assist anyone who would like help in preparing the lists.

Before adjournment, a follow-up meeting should be scheduled eight or nine days hence. Advise staff members that they will be called on to present and discuss their lists at that follow-up meeting. (This second meeting should be scheduled as soon after the list submission date as possible. That is, the time elapsed should be only that needed by you to duplicate and become familiar with the information turned in.)

As these key personnel present their listed items at the follow-up meeting(s), attempt, through synergistic discussion, to come up with wordings and dollar amounts that are clear and acceptable to all. Similarly, attempt to quantify in dollars requested items presented without a price tag.

In some organizations, the executive in charge may

find it difficult to maintain an atmosphere of cooperation and professionalism at these follow-up meetings. In cases where some staff members take offense at the expressed needs of others, you may be required to steer the meeting back to its intended tone and purpose. Keep in mind that if the needs of each function were already being satisfied, a turnaround would probably not be required. This needs list step is important and should be pushed to completion with simple, straightforward references to its value, as well as to the critical necessity for teamwork.

The final internal needs summary, after it has been hammered out at the follow-up meeting and edited by you or your delegate, should be put into a form similar to that shown in Figure 8. All items needed by each function should be categorized according to the other functions from which they are needed. All needs must be recorded twice in this summary listing, once as a "Needed by" and once as a "Needed from." For example, items listed as needed by Marketing from Engineering in the Marketing section shown in Figure 8 would also be listed in the Engineering section as needed from Engineering by Marketing.

A quick perusal of the completed summary will provide you with some answers to the following important questions:

1. In what function, or subsection of a function, are the noted opportunities for earnings improvement the greatest? On the "by" side? On the "from" side? What might this indicate about the person(s) responsible for those functions?
2. Do the "bys" and "froms" balance from side to side? Why? Shouldn't they?
3. Which function seems to have done the best job in quantifying its needs? Have those functions listing only minor items overlooked some major opportunities?
4. Which staff members have already initiated ac-

Figure 8. Internal needs summary form.

	Date _____
	Page _____ of _____
Internal Needs Summary	
Needed by <u>Marketing</u> from <u>Engineering</u>	Needed from <u>Marketing</u> by <u>Engineering</u>
1.	1.
2.	2.
.	.
.	.
.	.
Needed by <u>Marketing</u> from <u>Accounting</u>	Needed from <u>Marketing</u> by <u>Accounting</u>
1.	1.
2.	2.
.	.
.	.
.	.

tions to reduce the number of items needed from them?

5. How does the internal needs summary compare with the functional audit? Do the functions rated strongest and weakest in the functional audit have either the shortest or longest "by" or "from" needs lists?

In situations where heads of functions are the same persons who were there at the time of the functional audit, the turnaround manager might be suspicious if the function audited as strongest receives the longest list of items needed from it and/or if the function audited as weakest has the shortest such list. All other combinations tend to support the validity of the functional audit and internal needs list, but should be compared in order to arrive at reasons for the apparent agreement among the extremes found in each of these evaluations.

The completed needs list should then be filed with the other assessment information, for later use in constructing the final summaries, which will in turn become the basis for future planning.

Corporate Opportunities

Now for the last step in the assessment process, one final pass at suggestions from key subordinates concerning the best short-range opportunities for the company. These recommendations will differ from the internal needs list because they are not directed at items required from other functions of the business and because they are corporation-wide.

This final phase should be introduced at the internal needs follow-up meeting as an opportunity for the staff to add the finishing touches to assessing where the company stands at present. At this session, request that each functional head submit a list of company problems and opportunities within two weeks. The heads should include those items that offer the greatest financial return and that can be accomplished in less than a year.

These suggestions should be submitted in the simple format of five or six clear statements of opportunities, each followed by its estimated annual financial return, if realized.

The following information is not required at this time, but because it will be needed at some later date, remind your staff to think about alternative means, time frames, implementation costs, people to be in charge, and means for measuring performance relative to each of their submitted suggestions.

As soon as possible after the lists of opportunities have been submitted, categorize them by function and then mold them into consensus form at a staff meeting.

Assessment Summary

Seven assessment inputs are now available:

1. Financial inventory.
2. Functional audit.
3. Evaluation of key employees.
4. Feedback from key outside contacts.
5. Internal needs list.
6. Corporate opportunities list.
7. Record of other improvements already underway or completed.

It is time to turn these assessment inputs into potential objectives. This should be done in a summary form, conducive to use in the planning and execution steps about to be undertaken in the following sequence: (1) short-range planning, (2) implementation of a management control system, and (3) strategic long-range planning.

In order to best facilitate the accomplishment of these oncoming tasks, it is recommended that all items demanding or suggesting action (shortcomings, problems, opportunities) be transposed to two cross-referenced summary forms. Only elements that may be shared with key subordinates are to be included in these summaries. Those few elements of a more confidential nature, such as a planned personnel change, are best transferred to a third, confidential summary, for the sole use of the executive in charge.

First, the items to be included should be summarized under the respective corporate function most closely associated with them. Each function, or department, should be assigned a code letter so that, if "E" designates Engineering, the first item listed under the Engineering function would be potential objective E01, and so forth. If the objective is revised, a letter code could be added; for example, the first revision of objective E01 would be E01-A.

In some cases, potential objectives may border on several functional areas. Accurate bills of material, for example, may be listed as E01, because Engineering has the primary responsibility for them. But they may also involve considerable work from both MIS and Production Planning in their construction and maintenance. If this is the case, and the summary listing does not become too long, it would be wise to list objective E01 at the ends of both the MIS and Production Planning sections.

Whenever the information is readily available, the estimated annual pretax gain (reward) should be noted beside each item on the list.

The second summary is basically a clerical task, picking off each statement with its designated alphanumeric code and estimated reward in the order in which it appears on the first summary and inserting it under the appropriate one of three headings on the second. The three headings are: To Increase Sales, To Reduce Costs or Expenses, and To Improve Human or Organizational Relationships.

With the results from the individual assessment procedures and the two summaries completed and available, you are now ready to embark on a formal short-range improvement program.

9
Establish and Set Priorities for Short-Range Objectives

ALMOST half of this book has been devoted to means by which you, the executive responsible for a business turnaround, can assess your company's current situation.

This exhaustive treatment was designed for good purpose. First and foremost, the turnaround structure, like a large building, requires an especially strong and well-engineered foundation. In effect, you have been analyzing the soil conditions, weather extremes, space requirements, local ordinances, traditions, financial needs, and so forth, that apply to your turnaround structure.

Just as important, however, is that most businesses in need of a turnaround are in that position because of an unidentified flaw in one or more of the basics of doing business. Even in those cases where a major weakness might be outmoded equipment, as is the case with some airlines, the real cause can usually be traced back to a basic flaw in the equipment replacement policy. The purpose of the assessment procedures prescribed here is to assure a broad assessment, with a multidimensional view of each basic function. By following these procedures, you not only clearly identify every function but also examine each one from several different viewpoints.

Third, I want to kill a practice that is common to

most businesses requiring a turnaround. Very often these companies continue to follow the same practices that caused the original failures. They leap without looking onto one panacean bandwagon after another, with no comprehensive evaluations of their real weaknesses. As these firms devote the majority of their time and effort to each newfound cure-all, less and less time becomes available to correct their basic weakness(es). Thus further deterioration occurs.

A final reason for such a comprehensive preliminary analysis has to do with the fact that the key to the growth and success of the business is a very comprehensive, creative, long-range strategic plan. Each of the seven assessment steps taken thus far will play a necessary role in the formulation of that plan.

However, before embarking on long-range strategy, two independent interim action steps are strongly recommended.

The first of these steps, which will be discussed later in this chapter, is a short-range action plan designed for immediate earnings improvement. The second interim action step, to which the next three chapters are devoted, is the development and implementation of control systems, which are essential to the effectiveness of all plans. These controls include a vibrant management with objectives program, meaningful budgets, and other control formats designed to measure performance and to keep the formal short- and long-range programs on schedule.

The short-range improvement program serves several valuable purposes:

1. It provides an exciting and enjoyable head start, leading into the long-range program. Success breeds success. Nothing can beat going into long-range planning sessions with a confident and enthusiastic staff, looking forward to catching the big fish, having already accomplished significant savings within a short period of time. The members of your staff will sense that the turnaround

is already under way and that they have been, and will be, instrumental in a continued surge upward.

2. To some degree, the short-range program is similar to a shakedown cruise. Crew members will be gaining experience in all skills needed for the long trip. The captain will have an opportunity to observe their individual strengths and weaknesses in action and to modify plans for the long haul accordingly.

3. The major benefit of a successful short-range program is most often the profit improvement and the generation of additional cash that results from it. To be successful, the program must bring about sufficient financial improvement to make insiders and outsiders alike sit up and take notice. Show them that it can be done, and strongly convey that this is only the beginning. A new breath of life will be inhaled by employees, who will increase their work efforts. Stockholders, corporate officers, bankers, and others will sense a much lower risk in applying their funds to the company. Earnings gained from the short-range program will breed increased investment of effort and money in the long-range program to come.

List Meaningful Short-Range Objectives

The short-range plan must include specific goals that can be accomplished in less than a year (preferably in six months) and that will produce significant immediate financial returns and/or refit the enterprise for larger financial gains over the next several years.

The first step in the short-range planning process is to list potential objectives. These objectives should include projects already in progress, as well as all items from the internal needs summary that can be accomplished with minimal effort, and a group of opportunities selected from the various assessment procedures just completed. The final plan should be limited to about a dozen items in order to avoid a short-range program that is too cumbersome.

Although the prime objective is to seek projects with the greatest financial return, involvement must also be a major consideration. If at all practical, every staff member, or functional head, should be responsible for at least one project. No one should be involved to the degree that the value of accomplishment will be outweighed by the value of time sacrificed from regular duties. Some trade-offs, such as a project assignment in a functional area other than one's own, may be necessary to strike the best balance between financial return and involvement.

Specific short-range objectives, other than those already being acted upon and those listed as internal needs, may be selected in one of several ways: (1) You can make the choice unilaterally. (2) Copies of the entire assessment list by function can be distributed to the staff with instructions for each member to select several in his or her own field with the greatest potential six-month financial return. Or (3) you may meet individually with each of your subordinates and together choose a few select objectives from the functional responsibility of each.

I prefer the third alternative because of the opportunity it provides to individually enthuse subordinates between group planning sessions.

If this third route is taken, the "by" and "from" internal needs pertaining to that person's function should also be discussed at this private meeting. The purpose in this is to reach a preliminary decision on which needs will, and will not, be accepted as part of the short-range program. Include only goals whose potential gain definitely exceeds the cost of fulfilling the need. Often, this decision must be yours alone, especially in cases of conflict between the "needed by" and the "needed from" functions.

Following this preparatory course, hold a short staff

meeting to launch the short-term internal needs satisfaction program—covering which needs will be included, who is responsible for doing what, the deadline
for completion, and how frequently progress will be reviewed. It should be realized that the adopted program
may be subject to one final modification. The time and
effort required to achieve a major savings from carrying
out the short-range objectives program might necessi-
tate an approved delay of an element or two in the internal needs program.

Brainstorm Alternative Courses of Action

After the tentative short-range objectives have been selected, you should do three things:

1. Call a Saturday staff meeting for the purpose of
   establishing the formal short-range planning
   program. A meeting of approximately eight hours
   should be sufficient.
2. Distribute a copy of the tentatively agreed upon
   short-range objectives to each member of the staff,
   advising them to come to the meeting prepared
   to brainstorm alternative means for achieving
   each objective, to estimate viable time schedules
   for each, to recommend a person responsible for
   each, to estimate costs, to estimate financial returns, and to suggest controls that will assure
   performance to schedules.
3. Assign someone the task of designing a form similar to that shown in Figure 9, having sufficient
   copies made, and listing one of the selected objectives at the top left of each copy.

When the staff meets, it is recommended that work
sheets not be distributed, but that instead you record
pertinent points on a single copy retained by the chair.
If the facilities are available, a transparency of the work

Figure 9. Short-range objectives work sheet.

Short-Range Objectives Work Sheet

Date _____

Page _____ of _____

Objective _____

Estimated annual pretax return _____

Alternative Means of Accomplishment	Resources Needed	Selected Alternative	Estimated Cost to Implement	No. of Weeks to Complete	Target Completion Date	Person in Charge	Estimate Annual Pretax Reward	Controls Necessary to Assure Scheduled Attainment
a.								
b.								
c.								
d.								

sheet, with comments as they are added, could be projected for all to see. It is also often worthwhile to have a secretary present to record comments that may be extraneous to this meeting but of value at a later date.

Alternative means for achieving the stated objectives should be the first order of business, in order to complete the brainstorming activity while everybody is still fresh.

In order to encourage alternative means for accomplishing each objective, begin by going through the forms, sheet by sheet. The first column should be completed on all forms, before any other columns are addressed.

Because this is a brainstorming session, the staff members should be encouraged to offer any ideas that enter their minds and to offer new, revised, or combined objectives. Also, if they are inspired with a new thought or question about a previously discussed objective, they should be permitted to request an immediate return to the relevant sheet.

After the brainstorming session, the staff should be very optimistic about the possibilities that lie ahead. Usually this is the point where a significant increase in enthusiasm begins to take hold.

After the post-brainstorming break, or lunch, one final pass should be made to sharpen and polish the objectives and alternative means for achieving them.

Formalize the Short-Range Program

Next comes the step of selecting the objectives that are to be included in the formal program and the one or several alternative methods to be used in achieving each one.

This can best be accomplished through synergistic discussion of those alternatives and other columns of the work sheets as they apply to each alternative. Some opportunities may be decided on the basis of resource availability, cost or time of implementation, cost-effectiveness, availability of the proper person to put in charge, work overload, and so forth. Some might be tabled for lack of valid measuring or control tools. Others may be postponed, to be included later in the long-range program.

Generally, the task of selection is simple. The business needs a turnaround; the turnaround needs rapid energizing; the opportunities presented on the work sheets should spark more than enough energy to do the job. As a matter of fact, one valid method of selection is to choose the alternatives that are easiest to accomplish, making certain that they total more than the minimum amount necessary to show a marked improvement on the income statement.

Be sure to accomplish the intended task without spreading your people too thin. Maintain their availability for other, upcoming turnaround assignments.

Two samples of completed work sheets are shown in Figures 10 and 11. Each represents a typical, and simple, actual case.

The company involved in Figure 10 produces very sensitive products with complex chemical structures. From almost every source in the assessment procedures, the chief executive was reminded of one product line with a traditional scrap and spoilage level of 70 percent. After discussing the subject with his key subordinates, he was convinced that a 90 percent yield was not beyond reasonable expectation. If that level of yield were consistently achieved, the business would gain $500,000 a year through cost reduction and profits from new business.

Thus objective "Q02—Reduce scrap level from 70 % to 10 % on Product CDO-1" was born.

At the Saturday review meeting, the product manager for CDO-1 first suggested in-process inspections as a way of obtaining the stated objective. However, the quality assurance manager immediately countered, saying that inspectors cannot inspect quality into a

Figure 10. Completed short-range objectives work sheet.

Short-Range Objectives Work Sheet

Date 2/15

Page ____ of ____

Objective OO2—Reduce scrap level from 70% to 10% on product CDO-1

Estimated annual pretax return $500,000 ($200,000 cost reduction, $300,000 operating income on new sales)

Alternative Means of Accomplishment	Resources Needed	Selected Alternative	Estimated Cost to Implement	No. of Weeks to Complete	Target Completion Date	Person in Charge	Estimate Annual Pretax Reward	Controls Necessary to Assure Scheduled Attainment
a. Add in-process inspection and testing after each critical operation.								
b. Require supervisors to adhere to established processes, setups, and routings.								
c. Require expediters to assure first-in, first-out flow of product through each department. Require all spoilage and scrap to be moved immediately to designated scrap collection area.								
d. (1) Revalidate processes and tolerances. (2) Implement first-in, first-out processing flow controls.. (3) Require supervisors to remove all scrap to scrap area, and to follow established processes.	3-week engineering study to validate processes. Possibly new process controls and some equipment.	X	$75,000, if control equipment is needed	6	5/1	(1) J. Wilkerson (2) W. Maupay (3) W. Maupay	$500,000	Validation task list and weekly time schedule by 3/1 (J. Wilkerson). Sequential lot number first-in, first-out control by 4/1 (W. Maupay). Twice/shift walk-through checks to see that all scrap is in scrap area by 4/1 (W. Maupay). Supervisors sign route sheets indicating compliance with approved process by 3/15 (D. Smith). Monthly product line profit and loss reports to evaluate financial return (C. Blair).

product after it has been ruined. He suggested that all that was needed was for production supervisors to adhere to established processes, setups, and routings. The engineering manager said he believed a major part of the problem was a lack of inventory control over the product, which had a very limited in-process shelf life. He suggested that the objective could be achieved merely by having expediters to assure first-in, first-out rapid flow through the intermediate operations. Finally, the plant manager added his piece. His supervisors had informed him that the specified temperature and ingredient-blending tolerances were too loose and that their speed and temperature controls could not be fine-tuned to meet the tighter tolerances that should be specified. He had personally observed batches made as prescribed, which had turned out defective. He further accepted responsibility for his supervisors' not following established procedures and for allowing material to build up in some cases. But he ascribed these shortcomings to their efforts to meet production schedules by attempting to resurrect some products already known to be defective.

The executive in charge decided: (a) to have the critical processes and process control equipment revalidated, (b) to implement a first-in, first-out in-process inventory flow, with an established maximum inventory to be permitted in each department at any one time, (c) to require that all defective material be moved immediately upon discovery to clearly marked scrap areas within each department, and (d) to hold supervisors responsible for following established processes to the letter.

The engineering manager and the plant manager agreed that new process controls, if needed, could probably be purchased and installed for $65,000. To allow for the cost of the process study, a total estimated cost of $75,000 was noted on the work sheet.

It was believed that the program itself could be completed in six weeks. The target completion date was set for an additional five weeks or so away in order to allow some leeway for slippage.

The name of the person in charge of each phase was noted on the work sheet.

In order to avoid drawing out the length of this Saturday meeting, it is recommended, in regard to the last column of Figure 10, that during the session you merely obtain commitments that the necessary controls can and will be made available, rather than discussing how the controls will be developed. This was done for objective Q02 at this meeting.

Then, early the following week, the general manager met with the engineering manager and accepted his suggestion that by March 13 he submit a scheduled task list for the revalidation project and submit weekly performance-to-schedule reports thereafter until the project was completed. Later on in the week, the quality assurance manager advised that he would assume responsibility for produce flow and scrap removal, by means of sequential lot numbering and twice-per-shift departmental walk-throughs by his roving inspectors. He added that this would result in no additional cost. Knowing that something was being done to improve the processes and process controls, the plant manager enthusiastically agreed to accept responsibility for having his supervisors sign each shop order form to indicate full compliance with established procedures.

Although the company did not formally report profits by product line, the general manager was aware, from previous discussions, that the controller had been informally tracking monthly losses on product CDO-1 because of its unprofitability. The controller was only too glad to offer to continue this practice, forwarding a copy of her report to the general manager on a monthly basis. She knew that the success of this one project would result in an obvious improvement in the company's monthly earnings report.

(For those interested in the outcome of this project,

the engineers discovered a series of interactive relationships between time, temperature, and ingredient levels, as well as faulty and inadequate process control equipment. The equipment needed to correct the problem cost over $70,000 and would require four months to deliver and install. But within eight months the profit and loss report on product CDO-1 showed a monthly pretax improvement of over $20,000. Furthermore, unit costs dropped for all other products in the involved production departments as the result of the disappearance of this major confusion factor.)

In the case exemplified in Figure 11, the sales manager was convinced that he could immediately gain a 20 percent increase in profitable business if delivery integrity could be raised from its current 40 percent level to over 90 percent. The staff concurred but thought the project was too complex to be considered short range. The three production superintendents felt that the goal could not be realized with the recently implemented production control system, and suggested a return to the old way of doing things (alternative *a*). They also suggested that new and revised products were being introduced to production too rapidly and too haphazardly, often being promised for delivery before new tooling was procured and tested (alternative *b*).

The controller recommended a change in the on-time delivery bonus program for supervisors. The three production superintendents had been receiving a bonus of 5 percent of their monthly base salary whenever their dollar shipments directly to customers exceeded 90 percent of those scheduled for the month. Two problems were inherent in that program: (1) No consideration was given to individual orders; only dollar volume was considered. Small orders and small sections of large orders were thus frequently overlooked. (2) Although the superintendents each shipped directly to customers from their own departments, they were all heavily dependent on receiving in-process materials and parts from the other superintendents in order to make their customer

Figure 11. Completed short-range objectives work sheet.

Short-Range Objectives Work Sheet

Date _____ 2/15 _____
Page _____ of _____

Objective S03—Increase complete and on-time deliveries from 40% to 90% of all orders shipped

Estimated annual pretax return _____ Estimated annual pretax return _____ $800,000 operating income from 20% increase in business

Alternative Means of Accomplishment	Resources Needed	Selected Alternative	Estimated Cost to Implement	No. of Weeks to Complete	Target Completion Date	Person in Charge	Estimated Annual Pretax Reward	Controls Necessary to Assure Scheduled Attainment
a. Replace new production control system with system used before.								
b. Slow down rate of product innovation to level that can effectively be absorbed by Manufacturing. Temporarily suspend all product changes.	None	X	None	1	3/15	J. Wilkerson	$200,000	Sales manager alect all sales personnel and customers of temporary restriction to take effect with orders received after 3/15. All internal department heads to be informed of this directive immediately.
c. Change supervisory bonus system for on-time deliveries.	Weekly report of interdepartmental deliveries to schedule, in form similar to that reporting outside deliveries. Similar weekly report of interdepartmental complaints and returns.	X	$18,000/yr	2	4/1	C. Blair	$400,000 (Estimate this will achieve half of total goal.)	Weekly report of satisfactory, complete, and on-time deliveries by both the number and value of orders. Monthly report from controller of estimated return.
d. Provide accurate, updated bills of material in a form convenient for use by Manufacturing.								

shipments. In that no bonus credit was given for inter-departmental shipments, these were often sacrificed in order to meet the bonus requirements on direct-to-customer shipments.

The controller recommended a bonus program that she offered to monitor on a weekly basis (alternative *c*). It was based on the percentage of specific orders, inter-departmental as well as direct to customers, that were shipped complete and on time each week. The production superintendents would be paid a monthly bonus on a sliding scale up to 10 percent of their salary, for delivery performance of from 85 percent to 95 percent, and the 12 first-line supervisors would receive a 5 percent monthly bonus whenever the overall delivery integrity of their departments exceeded 90 percent.

Finally, the data processing manager made a plea for accurate, updated bills of material as the major means for achieving the stated objective (alternative *d*).

The general manager immediately tabled alternatives *a* and *d* as being too long range. The bills-of-material program required a complete overhaul before it could be a viable tool for all functions. The old production control program was totally dependent on the memories of two senior schedulers and would be a disaster without both of them on board.

It was decided that a temporary moratorium would be put on all product changes until those already in the pipeline could be effectively assimilated by Manufacturing. And the general manager decided to take a gamble and accept the bonus brainstorm of the controller. Target completion dates were set, taking into account that in addition to the number of weeks needed to complete the project, there would be lag time in notifying customers and getting out reports.

The general manager's judgment was sound. Within 60 days over 90 percent of all orders were being delivered complete and on time, and within 90 days new orders were flowing in at a 20 percent higher rate.

Staff members should not have to be reminded of

this, but remind them anyway when assigning responsibilities and establishing time schedules: All involved are expected to accept and complete these short-range objectives as scheduled, without any sacrifice or slippage in their other assignments, unless authorized at this planning session. If a member of the staff believes he or she cannot meet this requirement, that person should state this immediately. In almost every case, a satisfactory solution can be reached, wherein the person abandons or delegates some duty of lesser importance.

Before adjourning the meeting, remind those in attendance of the red flag and short daily meeting techniques (discussed in Chapter 1) to avoid program detours often imposed by daily emergencies. In addition, repeat the rule of no excuses being acceptable unless presented sufficiently in advance of scheduled due dates to allow corrective action to be taken.

Implement the Short-Range Program

The officially adopted short-range program should then be summarized in writing, and a set of simple weekly control reports that apply solely to this program should be devised. Where confidentiality presents no problem, the summary program can be distributed to each member of the staff. The routine weekly control reports of progress should be submitted to a central source by those assigned the responsibility for their preparation. That central source should then immediately construct the project report package and distribute it as you direct.

A review of that package, including discussion of problems and accomplishments, should then become part of the agenda of weekly staff meetings, at least until the short-range program is well under way.

Finally, another basic precept of management can be expected to have an accelerative effect on the program. Problem situations tend to improve temporarily for no other reason than that they are receiving management attention. Therefore, don't be surprised to discover some marked improvements even before the accepted solutions have been implemented. On the other hand, do not deter or abort any projects because of this phenomenon, for it is most often only temporary. Situations will slip back to "normal" as attention fades, unless your planned improvement program is implemented.

10

Establish and Maintain an Integrated MWO Program

THE function of management is to convert investment to profit. Although this may sound simple, the conversion process is usually quite complex. Fortunately several techniques have been developed, proven, and refined over the years that can catalyze this investment-to-profit conversion for very long periods of time.

One of these techniques, the presence of an ongoing, sound, strategic long-range planning program was mentioned earlier and will be discussed in greater detail in Chapter 13.

Another of these techniques has come to be known as MBO, or management by objectives. I take strong exception to this term for the simple reason that all effective managing must be done by people, by managers. Managers are expected to work with certain tools, such as objectives, but the tools themselves cannot be expected to convert investment to profit. Thus I prefer to use the term management by managers with objectives, or MWO.

Most businesspeople have read enough on the subject of personal development and corporate success to be able to quickly state a number of reasons why, and situations where, MWO works—from the value of a road map to the success stories of individual titans and great corporations.

Not only did the individuals involved in those testimonials have specific goals firmly fixed in their minds, but through discipline from themselves or their supervisors, they were held responsible for achieving them.

Very few companies in need of a turnaround have viable MWO programs. I have yet to find one, even though leading management authorities classify this practice as a necessary managerial technique.

Therefore, it seems logical that a company in need of a turnaround that is not using one of the necessary managerial techniques would find its chances of success enhanced if it did so. And this is surely the case.

This chapter is devoted to a what, why, where, who, when, and how review of a typical, unsophisticated MWO program, ending with some discussion of ways to apply it to a turnaround program.

Many excellent books and seminars are available on the subject of MBO programs. Readers are encouraged to further develop their knowledge of this subject by utilizing such resources at some later date, for purposes of improving and sophisticating the program then in effect. However, it is recommended that the initial program be of a simple, introductory nature in order to minimize the time and paperwork involved and to avoid bogging down the turnaround program.

A review and discussion of this chapter at a staff meeting, which includes a short practice session devoted to writing individual objectives, should be sufficient to get a viable MWO program under way.

What Is MWO?

MWO is short for management by managers with objectives. It is a system of management in which managers and the individuals to whom they directly report:

1. Jointly establish goals and objectives for the subordinate manager.
2. Agree on a specific completion date for each established goal or objective.
3. Set means for measuring performance to these goals and objectives.
4. Review performance measures periodically to determine progress to date.
5. Take corrective action as necessary to keep progress on schedule.

In most areas of human performance, two critical elements for success are understanding and commitment. For MWO to work effectively, the people involved must understand the system and must be committed to their goals and objectives.

Two factors that tend to inhibit the success of MWO programs are dictatorial supervision and poorly selected performance measurements.

In order for the system to receive the necessary level of commitment, subordinate managers must be given a reasonable degree of leeway in selecting both their objectives and the means of measuring performance to those objectives. Means of measurement must be the minimal necessary to adequately measure and control performance. Less would be meaningless. Overly sophisticated means of measurement usually lead to two problems: excessive paperwork and an undue commitment to the performance reporting itself rather than to the objective.

Objectives must meet a number of criteria for the MWO program to be most effective. All goals must:

1. Be specific, measurable, and in written form.
2. Clearly define the final results that are to be achieved.
3. Be presented in order of their priority.
4. Be challenging.
5. Include a balanced menu of short-range, long-

range, routine, problem-solving, innovative, and
personal objectives.

6. Be integrated with overall organizational needs,
   be consistent with corporate planning, and be established so that when achieved, they will support achievement of higher-level goals. For this
   reason, gaps and overlaps need to be avoided. The
   MWO goals structure should be established so that
   when all individual goals are achieved, the goals
   of the company will also be met.

7. Be communicated to everyone involved in the
   program.

Why MWO?

MWO has several distinct advantages to support its use,
other than those mentioned earlier in this chapter:

1. There has been a direct correlation between corporate MWO usage and staying in the Fortune 500
   during the past 40 years.

2. Intuition is replaced by objective management
   because objectives are clearly defined and measurable.

3. MWO utilizes an action mode rather than a reaction mode. Those involved make things happen according to an integrated plan, instead of
   reacting to happenstance.

4. MWO provides for the accomplishment of extremely complex objectives, through the accomplishment of a series of simpler, supportive goals.

One closing comment on the "whys" of MWO to those
who think they tried it before and weren't satisfied with
it: It is extremely important to carefully define what was
tried and why it wasn't satisfactory before condemning
the technique. If implemented as outlined in this chap-

ter, and as part of the overall program described in this book, MWO will be an extremely effective management tool.

The Where, Who, and When of MWO

Any company in need of a turnaround should consider implementing an MWO program at this point in its turnaround schedule. Short-range objectives, ideal for kicking off an MWO program, have just been established.

In most instances, to be most effective, an MWO system should eventually include all exempt salaried personnel. However, many MWO programs work extremely well when limited to those individuals who have other employees reporting to them.

Care should be exercised to not move the program down the organizational levels too rapidly. Managers should be given sufficient time to develop skills and build an effective program at one organizational level before MWO is extended to the next lower level. In an organization with a quarterly MWO program, where objectives are formally established at the beginning of each quarter, a good rule of thumb is to move the program down one level of management no more frequently than once every six months.

When to begin? Those reporting directly to the executive in charge of the turnaround should be included as soon as possible. Ask them to present their suggested goals for the next fiscal quarter by the 15th of the month preceding the start of that quarter.

Then a schedule should be distributed to everyone who eventually will be included, noting the date when each will be brought into the program. That schedule should also provide for group training sessions two to four weeks prior to each inclusion date.

The How of MWO

As noted earlier in this chapter, MWO systems vary from elementary simplicity to extreme sophistication. Although the more complex systems do offer certain advantages such as "fail-safe" features, a simple program is strongly recommended in turnaround circumstances. A basic MWO program will result in attainment of the few major goals needed immediately and will not deter the participants from learning the various other techniques required to bring about the turnaround.

No matter what type of MWO system is chosen, the ingredients remain the same:

1. Objectives for each subordinate manager.
2. Targeted completion dates for each objective.
3. Means for measuring performance to each objective.
4. Regular periodic reviews of progress.
5. Corrective action as needed to keep progress on schedule.

Most MWO programs include four basic types of objectives with which each manager works:

1. Routine objectives, which provide stability.
2. Problem-solving objectives, designed to correct known flaws in functional performances.
3. Innovative objectives, which provide for earnings growth.
4. Personal objectives, intended to develop the skills of the manager involved.

A good set of objectives from any one manager will contain a blend of these four types.

Objectives should be formally established by an interactive discussion between a manager and his or her immediate superior, subsequent to a good deal of preparatory work on the part of the manager, and after the manager has had time to review the objectives tentatively proposed. In other words, subordinate managers submit to their superiors lists of tentative objectives to be accomplished within the established time period. The superiors review these proposals and edit and add to them as they deem advisable. At this point, each superior also compares all proposals received from his or her subordinates, to make certain that together they will accomplish the overall objectives for which that superior is responsible, and modifies individual proposals as needed to achieve this end.

Subordinate managers are then called in individually by their superiors to discuss their proposals. By dialogue, final agreement is reached and approved objectives are established. These finalized objectives are then photocopied and distributed by the superiors to their immediate subordinates who are involved in the program.

The next section of this chapter presents a series of standard guidelines for use by subordinate managers in choosing and stating their tentative objectives. You should pass on these guidelines to your immediate subordinates at a meeting dedicated to introducing your MWO program.

At this point in the turnaround program, the suggestions offered for selecting objectives are not as important as they will become in the future. This is because most of the managers' objectives for the quarter immediately ahead have already been selected for them as a result of the previously adopted internal needs list and short-range objectives program. However, these managers should be required to include at least one personal objective in their proposals. They should also include any routine and problem-solving objectives they deem necessary. And to repeat, the objectives assigned to each from the mutual needs and short-range programs must be included.

On the other hand, this is an ideal time for staff members to get needed practice in the proper statement of MWO objectives. The executive in charge should be careful to accept only objectives that are properly and completely stated.

The Four Types of Objectives

Before discussing the steps usually followed in selecting and stating objectives, a short review of the four types of objectives is in order. These are: routine objectives, problem-solving objectives, innovative objectives, and personal objectives.

Routine Objectives

A routine objective involves the maintenance of an established critical function or procedure, without improving it. For example, if credit and accounts receivable management is already being handled adequately, the controller might decide to divert the time required to improve that function to the improvement of some other area that offers a more lucrative reward. In such a case, continued management of accounts receivable at no more than 40 days outstanding as reported in the monthly financial report, and at no additional cost, might be considered a routine objective for the controller.

The simplest technique for defining, measuring, and evaluating a routine objective is by exception. Activities that lend themselves best to control by exception reporting are considered routine for MWO purposes. Routine objectives don't require schedules, progress reports, or periodic activity reports. Activity should be reported only when an exception to the established standard occurs, that is, when it falls outside the limits set forth in the objective.

It should also be realized that an objective considered routine at one level of management may be placed in a different category at a subordinate level. The credit manager, for example, may offer a problem-solving objective that is very meaningful at that level and to which his time should rightfully be devoted even though his superior has listed credit management as a routine objective.

Problem-solving Objectives

A problem-solving objective is created when a routine practice either breaks down or proves inadequate. The establishment of routine objectives and the means for their measurement often leads to the identification of problem-solving objectives. In thinking about a routine, people conceive an idea for significant improvement and thus create an objective of this second type. On the other hand, one goal of problem-solving objectives is to transform the abnormal to the normal, and therefore to create additional routine objectives that can be managed by exception.

In order to establish a problem-solving objective, the manager must search for activities that are currently inconsistent with corporate objectives, and evaluate the difference between what should be accomplished and what actually is being done.

One trait of good managers is their ability to correctly set priorities for the problem-solving objectives in their areas, recognizing that not all problems can be solved simultaneously.

The construction of problem-solving objectives provides an excellent opportunity for in-depth discussions between managers and their subordinates. These talks with subordinates are often of significant value in further pinpointing areas of weakness and in separating business diseases from their symptoms. Occasionally, the problem presented by the subordinate as the basis for an objective is not the real problem at all, but the presentation and discussion lead to the identification of the real problem.

Innovative Objectives

Innovation has been called the lifeblood of industry. A manager should rightfully expect subordinate managers to offer the type of innovative objectives that will provide these subordinates with financial recognition and promotion. Frequently, the manager's innovative goals are in response to the needs of a higher managerial level. Yet, many times innovative objectives are nothing more than a creative expansion of routine activities that are currently considered satisfactory but that offer significant rewards for radical improvement. For example, a hospital administrator may be satisfied with her cost per patient day, because it is about average for that type and size institution. She lists maintenance of the current cost level as a routine objective, until she gets a brainstorm that may lower that cost by 5 percent. At that time, the routine objective becomes an innovative one.

Innovative goals are usually the most exciting, challenging, and difficult. Excitement goes hand in hand with creativity. All worthwhile achievements offer some form of challenge, but with innovative goals the challenge begins right at the start, in effectively stating the objective, in calculating the anticipated return on investment, and in convincing one's superior that it can be done. An element of difficulty comes into play when you are called on to reward the innovative performance of a subordinate. You must recognize that some employees have more of an opportunity to come up with innovative ideas simply because of the nature of their positions and that many successful innovations involve the concepts and efforts of more than one person. You should present a reward to an innovator only if you are positive that that person is singularly responsible and only if you have established a record for rewarding outstanding routine and problem-solving performance as well.

Personal Objectives

MWO can be very fruitful in managing one's personal life and career. Personal objectives might include the development of talents needed either to perform one's present job at the optimal level or to achieve a promotion and/or long-range goals related to the ultimate position to which one aspires.

In establishing personal goals, several items are very important:

1. An honest self-evaluation is essential. Otherwise goals will be too difficult to attain or too unrewarding to merit the time applied.
2. Well-planned, realistic short-range objectives will enable individuals to move toward their ultimate goal, through achievement of intermediate ones.
3. The measurable personal goals chosen should provide a blueprint and a schedule for success.

Selecting and Stating the Objectives

Each of the four types of objectives is best developed by subordinate managers according to the following three-step process. (Remember that originally the MWO goals are proposed by the subordinate managers.)

Step 1. Divide your total job into four to six key areas in which you want to set and meet objectives. Sometimes this has already been accomplished for you in your job specification, which lists the key areas of your responsibility.

For each area, record six or more answers to the question, "Where should I invest time and other resources?"

Beside each answer, note whether it represents a routine, problem-solving, innovative, or personal objective. Make certain you have at least one of each type of goal in your overall total.

Step 2. For each statement you have just written, identify at least two very specific measurable elements that can be monitored as indicators of performance.

Ask, "What should be available for someone to look at that will provide an assessment of my effectiveness in this area?"

Step 3. Next, translate each answer in Step 1 into an objective statement including:

    a. An accomplishment verb.
    b. A specific end result.
    c. The maximum investment in dollars, work hours, and/or sacrifice of performance in another area.
    d. The indicator from Step 2 to be used to measure performance.
    e. A completion date or time period.

To be an acceptable MWO objective, all five, and only these five, elements must be included.

In the case where an MWO program is being established early in a turnaround program, many of the tasks in Steps 1 and 2 will already have been done for managers. The majority of their objectives will already have been established. However, reducing them to acceptable form is not always an easy task and should therefore not be postponed until just prior to their due date. Subordinate managers should begin this three-step process as soon as possible after it has been assigned.

One closing comment in regard to the preparation of objectives. Note that objectives deal almost exclusively with *what* is to be done. The *how* is left very much to the discretion of the subordinate managers preparing them. In no way does this excuse the preparers from having given more thought to the *how* than to the *what*, nor from being prepared to discuss the *how* with their immediate superiors, upon request, at any time.

After this first set of objectives has been formally established and circulated to those involved, it is the

Figure 12. MWO summary sheet.

ZAB Corporation

Name ___C. Blair___ Qtr ___2___ 19___ Approved by ___R. Marcoux___

Position ___Controller___

Objective

Job Responsibility	Code	Accomplishment Verb	Specific End Result	Maximum Investment	Measure Progress by	Completion Date	
						Scheduled	Actual
Develops and installs coorporate financial procedures and controls to maintain a flow of information sufficient for adequate management control of the enterprise.	I	Issue	Monthly financial reports by the first Friday, instead of third Monday, of each fiscal month.	$10,000 software purchase. 40 hours to implement.	Weekly reports of progress to task by task schedule.	7/1	

Key: R. Routine I. Innovative S. Problem Solving P. Personal responsibility of the turnaround manager to monitor progress. This may be done in two ways. The routine reports, included as a part of each objective as its measuring device, must be read as received, and analyzed for discrepancies between actual and intended results. In every case where a discrepancy is reported, the person responsible for that objective must be immediately confronted, and a means for getting back on track decided upon. Weekly private individual meetings with all subordinates, including a short discussion of that person's MWOs will also uncover early warning signals. More important, the meetings will arouse these subordinates' interest in attaining their objectives, as a result of your attention to them.

This point in the program is often a good time to review and consolidate performance reports. The MWO program should have been integrated with all other short-range improvement programs to the degree that one MWO-oriented, uncomplicated set of performance/control reports can track all projects.

Also, at this time you should remind the members of your staff that their preliminary objectives for the following quarter will be due in your office 15 days prior to the beginning of that quarter.

Finally, an MWO system can be effectively integrated with a bonus or salary-increase program. Some preliminary thoughts might be applied to such a tie-in at this time, but it is best to wait a year before directly connecting the two.

A sample MWO form is shown in Figure 12.

You have now implemented the basic tools necessary to score some impressive short-range earnings improvements. The next chapter presents ways to use these tools to best advantage.

11
Achieve Short-Range Objectives

THE rapid attainment of short-term goals is an absolute necessity in a turnaround situation. A concerted effort must be made, not only to attain them but to attain them before their targeted due dates. Such an accomplishment will provide significant quantifiable financial and psychological leverage. If the proper objectives were selected, the proper controls implemented, and the overall objectives program managed properly and with total dedication, the results achieved will reach a level considered impossible at the onset of the program.

"How did you manage to do it? I can't believe it!"
"Sound, basic management!"

The short-range financial gains will have numerous positive repercussions. Directors and officers above the executive in charge of the turnaround will be impressed, and the purse strings of their capital investment bag will loosen. They will begin to form some new enthusiasm for the company. The fog will fade from their mental image of you as the person they chose to head the turnaround, and the turnaround will further benefit from their feeling of involvement and accomplishment. After all, they did select the right person to head it.

The financial improvement will also receive a strong favorable echo from creditors, if any are involved, who appreciate the real improvement of waiting less time for their money. Some bankers and suppliers will take their tongues out of their cheeks, put them back in the centers of their mouths, and be much more positive if and when future support is needed.

If the company is publicly held, the first quarterly report following completion of the short-range program might spark some price-raising stock trading. This point could also have excellent internal repercussions, if a number of employees hold stock in the company. I was involved in two companies in which a number of senior employees, including the turnaround manager's immediate superior, were long-time holders of stock that had been diminishing in value over the years before the turnaround effort. Their response to a quick rise in the stock price, reflecting the improved quarterly results of the short-term turnaround program, was an important factor in further accelerating an upturn in earnings growth.

Customers are almost always involved in some phase of the short-range program because increased sales is generally one of the objectives. Therefore, customers also will experience some degree of satisfaction as a result of the program's success.

When the short-range program is achieved ahead of schedule, and the results exceed those anticipated, an epidemic of enthusiasm among employees is to be expected. "We did it. Who said it couldn't be done? We won the league championship. Now let's go for the state title." What better frame of mind could you want for embarking on the major turnaround journey that lies just ahead? You know that you are prepared to keep the ball rolling, and now you have a cadre of subordinates who are anxious to help push it uphill.

Short-Range Objectives—The Three Keys to Success

It is extremely important to make a quick, significant score with the short-range program. The three keys to success of that program (assuming proper objectives were chosen and correctly specified in the first place) are involvement, control, and recognition.

Involvement

If you establish a short-range program, even one with a perfect set of bells and whistles, and then turn your attention to something else while waiting for your subordinates to accomplish their goals, you might as well forget the turnaround. The program may be completed to some degree, but with nowhere near the results that could have been achieved if you had continued to devote your time and energy to it.

As the leader of the program, you must exhibit continued sincere interest and encouragement. Don't let a chance encounter with anyone involved in the short-range program, regardless of that person's degree of involvement, pass without making a knowing comment or asking a question regarding that person's role in it. This is especially important with lower-echelon personnel. When they are aware that the "big boss" really does know what's going on at their level and sincerely cares, their performance miraculously improves. How do you react to a passing comment from one of your superiors? You take a quick trip back to the office and check that the item mentioned is, in fact, under control and at an acceptable level of performance, don't you? Then you make a daily follow-up, with an improvement of one type or another during the next several days. And, of course, you make a verifying phone call to the superior in question or a mental note to mention it the next time you meet, right?

You must, of course, involve yourself in the turnaround through formal means also. Careful attention to regular control reports of progress, and discussion of the current status and of any problems associated with each objective at regular meetings with staff and individual subordinates, are mandatory. Also, special meetings to resolve problems before they can jeopardize goal attainment are definitely in order.

Don't overlook the other side of the involvement coin: getting others involved. As many employees as possible should be included in the short-range program, so that as many as possible can feel that they have contributed to its success. Many of the stated objectives of the program will be conducive to division into individual tasks that, in turn, can be delegated downward through the organization. Usually, this is the most efficient way of accomplishing them. And most people prefer the sound of "I did it" and "We did it" to "She did it" or "They did it."

Develop the program and the people through involvement.

Control

The second element of a successful short-range program is control. Controls should serve a twofold purpose: They should measure actual progress against planned progress, and they should prevent program slippage by raising early warning signals whenever an objective is in danger of not being achieved on schedule.

Controls are absolutely necessary tools, but they are secondary in importance to the end they are designed to help achieve. As tools, they come in many forms: task-oriented controls such as Gantt, PERT, and CPM charts, as well as numerically oriented tools, such as tabulations and graphs. The key to choosing the best tool for controlling any given objective is to select the simplest format that will get the job done, make certain it is clearly understood by all involved, keep it current and accurate, and publish the results regularly according to a preestablished schedule.

Rapidly exploding computer technology has been an excellent contribution to control reporting. Much of the information needed for project control reporting is derived from data already in the computer data bank. With the proper software, the information can be retrieved from that bank in just about any form desired. However, this point merits a word of caution to the company just beginning to turn around. Unless the control data being sought are almost identical to some already being reported out of the computer, don't burden this resource with a control software project. Instead, manually construct and issue the short-range objectives control reports. They are short-range by definition and are prone to modification, and a number of more important computer programming projects are on the horizon.

Before discussing several basic types of control documents, I want to repeat the four ground rules for preventing projects from being detoured.

1. Accept nothing less than absolute integrity and teamwork.
2. Accept no excuses for not completing a project on time, unless the delay is brought to your attention sufficiently in advance of target due dates.
3. Insist that all unsolved daily emergencies that might delay the on-time attainment of any objective be reported to you within 24 hours of their discovery.
4. Positive thinking must prevail. Explain that negative opinions regarding any phase of the turnaround are not to be expressed to anyone, with one exception. Encourage anyone with a negative opinion to share it with you in private.

These ground rules alone will do much to bring about the success of the program.

Let's look now at some simple, effective control report forms, using the scrap reduction project noted in Chapter 9 as an example.

The objective in that case was to realize an annual pretax gain of $500,000 by reducing the scrap level of one product line from 70 percent to 10 percent. The goal was to be achieved by various means: an engineering study of processes and process controls, including recommendations for improvement; sequential numbering of batches of raw materials as they are entered into processing; immediate removal of scrap to designated scrap areas; supervisors initialing shop orders, certifying that they have followed the prescribed process in each case.

It was estimated that the project could be completed in six weeks at a cost of $75,000. The engineering manager was assigned the job of breaking down the project into individual tasks within two weeks, and a targeted completion date nine weeks hence was established.

Figure 13 shows the first control tool, the simple Gantt chart prepared by the engineering manager. It indicates that the project can be completed on schedule, at less than the anticipated cost, if available process controls can be repaired to consistently produce a product within tolerance. You'll notice that Judd Wilkerson was given about 2½ weeks for task 1, which actually took only one hour. This is often the case. Perhaps he anticipated that with all that was involved, the task would take a couple weeks. Then he procrastinated or had other things to do for a few days. When he actually started working on the task, he became enthused about it and completed it in an hour.

The general manager initials the control report and the project is undertaken. On Monday morning, March 14, the general manager receives a call from the engineering manager requesting a meeting that will include the plant manager and the maintenance superintendent.

At that meeting, the three subordinates advise the general manager that both the temperature and feed controls are defective and very old but could be repaired in approximately six weeks at a cost not to exceed $30,000. However, because of the extremely critical nature of the product and the large potential financial return, they recommend that two completely new sets of much more accurate controls be purchased at a total cost of $75,000, their delivery lead time being four months. The engineering manager presents the general

Figure 13. Preliminary schedule control chart for short-range objective Q02.

ZAB Corporation
Short-Range Objectives Program of 2/15/84

Goal ___ O02

Objective ___ Reduce scrap on product CDO 1 from 70% to 10%, saving $200,000/year and gaining $300,000 in annual pretax profits from increased sales.

Overall responsibility of ___ J. Wilkerson ___ Date ___ 2/15/84

Accurate, up-to-date copy of this form to ___ R. Marcoux ___ On ___ Each Monday a.m.

Task	Person Responsible	Week Ending Schedule	Cost Budget	Cost Actual	Comments
1. Chart tasks required to meet objective.	J. Wilkerson		Hrs 3 / $ 120	Hrs 1 / $ 40	
2. Check temperature, feed, and mixing controls.	P. Holmes		Hrs 40 / $ 920	Hrs / $	
3. Repair controls on weekends as needed.	G. Bender		Hrs 64 / $ 6,472	Hrs / $	Estimate $5,000 in parts and supplies needed.
4. Implement batch-numbering control.	P. Holmes		Hrs 3 / $ 90	Hrs / $	
5. Implement in-process flow and scrap removal controls.	W. Maupay		Hrs 6 / $ 120	Hrs / $	
6. Implement control of process verification by supervisor.	W. Maupay		Hrs 14 / $ 420	Hrs / $	
7. Verify tolerance levels of individual ingredients.	E. Miller		Hrs 30 / $ 900	Hrs / $	
8. Verify temperature tolerances.	R. Kloth		Hrs 30 / $ 900	Hrs / $	
9. Verify speed and feed tolerances.	F. Sturm		Hrs 30 / $ 900	Hrs / $	
10. Rewrite process specifications.	J. Wilkerson		Hrs 10 / $ 350	Hrs / $	
TOTAL PROJECT			Hrs 230 / $ 11,192	Hrs 1 / $ 40	Final comment

Initialed approval: RM RM

Special comments:

manager with a completed capital expenditure request form for these controls and a proposed revision in the schedule as shown in Figure 14. Not having authority to approve capital expenditures over $50,000, the general manager picks up the phone, calls the president, explains the urgency, and receives verbal approval to go ahead. He approves the revised project, and it is again under way.

Note that Figure 14 shows that tasks 4, 5, and 6 have already been completed. They, too, require controls to assure compliance, samples of which are shown in Figures 15–17.

Figure 15 deals with the sequential numbering of batches of product CDO-1. The plant manager has already issued a standard procedure instruction stating that it is the responsibility of the Melt Department supervisor to sequentially number each batch of material, to enter it in a daily log book, and to attach a specified type of identification tag to each batch, noting its number and the date and shift on which it was cast. The instruction further states that all department supervisors processing product CDO-1 are responsible for keeping the proper identification tag attached to the material at all times. A copy of the daily melt control log is shown in Figure 15.

Meanwhile, the quality assurance manager has issued two standard procedure instructions to his inspectors. The first, directed to roving inspectors, requires them, twice each shift, to make a walk-through inspection of all departments that process product CDO-1. They are to indicate, on the clipboard form provided, any unidentified batches of CDO-1, as well as any batches of CDO-1 that are *not* in the incoming storage racks, being processed on a machine, or in the designated scrap area. The instruction further requires the inspectors, upon discovering any such deviation, to immediately seek out and notify the departmental supervisor. The clipboard control form used for this purpose is shown in Figure 16.

Figure 14. Revised schedule control chart for short-range objective Q02.

Objective   Reduce scrap on product CDO-1 from 70% to 10%, saving $200,000/year and gaining $300,000 in annual pretax profits from increased sales.

Overall responsibility of   J. Wilkerson   Date   3/14/84

Accurate, up-to-date copy of this form to   R. Marcoux   On   Each Monday a.m.

Task	Person Responsible	Cost Budget	Cost Actual	%	Comments
1. Chart tasks required to meet objective.	J. Wilkerson	Hrs 3 / $ 120	Hrs 2 / $ 80		
2. Check temperature, feed, and mixing controls.	P. Holmes	Hrs 40 / $ 920	Hrs 21 / $ 483		Temperature and feed controls very old and defective. Can be repaired in 6 weeks for $30,000.
3. Repair controls on weekends as needed. A. Order receive, install new setup and feed controls.	G. Bender	Hrs 64 / $ 81,472	Hrs / $		Cannot be done in house. Revised 3/14/84.
4. Implement batch-numbering control.	P. Holmes	Hrs 3 / $ 90	Hrs 3 / $ 90		
5. Implement in-process flow and scrap removal controls.	W. Maupay	Hrs 6 / $ 120	Hrs 5 / $ 100		
6. Implement control of process verification by supervisor.	W. Maupay	Hrs 14 / $ 420	Hrs 16 / $ 480		Meeting with supervisors longer than expected.
7. Verify tolerance levels of individual ingredients. A. Rescheduled	E. Miller	Hrs 30 / $ 900	Hrs / $		
8. Verify temperature tolerances. A. Rescheduled	R. Kloth	Hrs 30 / $ 900	Hrs / $		
9. Verify speed and feed tolerances. A. Rescheduled	F. Sturm	Hrs 30 / $ 900	Hrs / $		
10. Rewrite process specifications. A. Rescheduled	J. Wilkerson	Hrs 10 / $ 350	Hrs / $		
TOTAL PROJECT		Hrs 230 / S 11,192	Hrs 47 / S 1,233 A. 230 / A. 86,192		Final comment

Week-Ending Schedule: 2/19, 2/26, 3/4, 3/12, 3/19, 3/26, 4/2, 4/9, 4/16, 4/23, 4/30, 5/7, 5/14, 5/21, 5/28, 6/4, 6/11, 6/18, 6/25, 7/1, 7/8, 7/15, 7/22, 7/29, 8/5, 8/12, 8/19, 9/2

Initialed approval: RM RM RM RM

Special comments: Received verbal approval from president on 3/14/84 to order $75,000 of new controls as specified on Capital Expenditure Request #8307. Ordered 3/14/84. Delivery promised before 7/8/84.

Figure 15. Daily melt control log form.

ZAB Corporation

Product No. _____

Date	Shift	Batch No.	Weight	No. of Pieces	Temp.	Feed	Comments	Clearly Initialed by

Figure 16. Batch flow and scrap removal control form.

ZAB Corporation

Product No. _____   Week Ending _____

Please note under Comments (and immediately notify production supervisor in charge) any subject material spotted at locations other than in material entry storage rack being processed at a machine, or in designated scrap area, as well as any material not bearing specified batch ID card.

Day	Shift	Time	Initial If OK	Comments	Name of Supervisor Notified
M	1				
M	2				
T	1				
T	2				
W	1				
W	2				
T	1				
T	2				
F	1				
F	2				
S	1				
S	2				
S	1				
S	2				

The second standard procedure instruction initiated by the quality assurance manager applies to final inspectors. It requires them to note the batch number and the name of the supervisors signing each shop order for product CDO-1, as well as to immediately notify their supervisors of any deviations, including sequential voids in batch numbers inspected. A sample copy of the final inspection control form is shown in Figure 17.

Completed copies of these three forms are submitted to the quality assurance supervisor on a daily basis for reconciliation.

This control procedure may seem extremely cumbersome, but it was deemed necessary in view of the $500,000 potential gain involved and the theretofore sloppy shop practices.

In the actual situation, it took nine months for all discrepancies to disappear from the combined control reports, and after one year only the melt log control was continued.

In addition to control reporting the input side of most short-range objectives, the output side of all short-range objectives promising a tangible return should be regularly and accurately recounted. Typical control reports on the outputs of the project are shown in Figures 18–21.

Figure 18 is a tabular presentation of the parameters involved in each project. It may seem extremely complex to the uninitiated, but it is not. Only one line is completed each week, and a reasonably qualified clerk can complete 12 sheets (12 projects) in less than two hours per week. Here is how the figures for each column were derived:

Columns A and B—The figures in these columns were posted by a clerk who took them directly from the Weekly Production Report.

Column C—These figures are quarter-to-date accumulations of the figures in column A. For example, the first number in column C, 39.1, was derived by adding the first two numbers in column A, 16.0 and 23.1.

Figure 17. Final inspection control form for short-range objective Q02.

ZAB Corporation

Product No. _____   Date _____ Inspector _____

Batch Number	Initials of Supervisor			Weight		No. of Pieces		Weight Rejected for Cause					Comment
	Dept. 3201	Dept. 3221	Dept. 3231	Good	Rejected	Good	Rejected	A	B	C	D	E	

Key: A. Temper   C. Tolerance   E. Discoloration
      B. Conductivity   D. Chemistry

ZAB Corporation

Weekly Activity Control Report

Short-range objective Q02-A—Reduce scrap level on product CDO-1

	A	B	C	D	E	F	G	H	I	J	K	L	M
	Lbs (000) This Week		Lbs (000) QTD		Actual % Scrap				Investment—QTD		Savings—QTD		Savings per P & L QTD
Week Ending	Good	Scrap	Good	Scrap	This Wk	Past 4 Wks	QTD	Goal QTD	Actual	Goal	Actual	Goal	
1/8	16.0	43.4			73		73	70		-0-	(173)		
15	23.1	43.8	39.1	88.2	66		69	70			141		
22	20.2	39.2	59.3	127.4	66		68	70			427		
29	20.3	39.3	79.6	166.7	66	68	68	70			572		
2/5	21.7	42.2	101.3	208.9	66	66	67	70			1,093		
12	21.3	47.5	122.6	256.4	69	67	68	70			882		
19	18.2	29.6	140.8	286.0	62	66	67	70		-0-	1,519		
26	14.1	18.6	154.9	304.6	57	65	66	70	80	120	2,228		
3/5	16.0	18.9	170.9	323.5	54	62	65	69	750	750	3,074	598	
12	19.3	21.7	190.2	345.2	53	57	64	68	1,233	1,670	4,105	1,332	
19	21.7	25.6	211.9	370.8	54	54	64	68	26,233	26,670	4,574	1,468	
26	13.3	14.9	225.2	385.7	53	54	63	67	26,233	26,670	5,669	2,406	
4/2	14.3	16.8	239.5	402.5	54	54	63	66	26,233	26,670	6,031	3,426	8,000
4/9	13.3	13.8	31.4	32.0	51	53	51	50		-0-	946	1,089	
16	18.1	18.2	53.0	57.3	50	52	50	50			2,262	2,447	
23	21.6	25.3	69.8	76.2	54	52	52	50			3,431	3,807	
30	16.8	18.9	91.9	97.5	53	52	52	50			4,520	5,166	
5/7	22.1	21.3	114.8	115.0	49	52	51	50			6,282	6,526	
14	22.9	17.5	133.9	134.1	43	50	50	50			8,258	7,885	
21	19.1	19.1	155.4	160.5	50	49	50	50			9,631	9,245	
28	21.5	26.4	173.9	175.6	55	50	51	50			10,622	10,605	
6/4	18.5	15.1	196.2	195.3	45	49	50	50			12,505	12,001	
11	22.3	19.7	218.1	220.1	47	50	50	50			14,112	13,143	
18	21.9	24.8	237.4	238.6	53	51	50	50	900		15,689	14,607	
25	19.3	18.5	254.3	254.8	49	49	50	50	900		17,076	16,108	
7/2	16.9	16.2			49	50	50	50	900	-0-	18,294	17,646	30,100

1st Qtr (weeks 1/8 – 4/2)

2nd Qtr (weeks 4/9 – 7/2)

Week Ending	Lbs (000) This Week Good (A)	Scrap (B)	Lbs (000) QTD Good (C)	Scrap (D)	Actual % Scrap This Wk (E)	Past 4 Wks (F)	QTD (G)	Goal QTD (H)	Investment—QTD Actual (I)	Goal (J)	Saving—QTD Actual (K)	Goal (L)	Savings per P&L QTD (M)
7/9	12.7	11.3			47	50	47	50			1,051	1,088	
16	16.1	13.1	28.8	24.4	45	48	46	50			2,483	2,447	
23	24.3	23.4	53.1	47.8	49	48	47	50	3,600	28,236	4,396	3,807	
30	13.5	16.4	66.6	64.2	55	49	49	50	4,000	31,472	5,028	5,166	
8/6	17.9	15.3	84.5	79.5	46	49	48	50	30,312	32,372	6,688	6,526	
13	16.8	5.6	101.3	85.1	25	46	46	50	31,212	33,272	8,748	7,885	
20	23.1	7.3	124.4	92.4	24	38	43	49	32,012	34,172	12,081	9,707	
27	22.1	4.5	146.5	96.9	17	29	40	49	32,012	59,522	15,809	11,135	
9/3	20.2	2.3	166.7	99.2	10	19	37	48	57,522	59,522	19,786	13,201	
10	17.9	1.3	184.6	100.5	7	16	35	47	57,522	59,522	23,243	15,114	
17	18.7	1.4	203.3	101.9	7	11	33	46	57,522	59,522	27,064	17,528	
24	19.0	1.5	222.3	103.4	7	8	32	45	57,972	59,522	30,390	20,135	
10/1	27.8	3.4	250.1	106.8	11	8	30	44	57,952	59,522	35,989	22,940	63,800
10/8	28.5	3.5			11	9	11	22		-0-	6,047	3,780	
15	28.2	1.8	56.7	5.3	6	9	9	20			12,447	7,968	
22	20.7	2.3	77.4	7.6	10	10	9	18			16,973	12,574	
29	28.1	2.8	105.5	10.4	9	9	9	16			23,144	17,609	
11/5	30.9	3.8	136.4	14.2	11	9	9	15			29,922	22,673	
12	24.4	2.7	160.8	16.9	10	10	10	14			34,711	28,013	
19	29.7	3.0	190.5	19.9	9	10	9	13			41,811	33,634	
26	18.3	3.2	208.8	23.1	15	11	10	13			45,060	36,748	
12/3	27.6	3.8	236.4	26.9	12	11	10	13			51,025	42,044	
10	21.6	3.2	258.0	30.1	13	12	10	12			55,687	48,278	
17	32.5	5.7	290.5	35.8	15	14	11	12			61,656	53,882	
24	18.6	2.6	309.1	38.4	12	13	11	12			65,594	58,436	
31	-0-	2.5	309.1	40.9	8	16	12	12		-0-	64,482	58,275	104,700

Rows 7/9 through 10/1 are bracketed as **3rd Qtr**; rows 10/8 through 31 are bracketed as **4th Qtr**.

Figure 18. Typical tabular weekly control report for a short-range objective.

Column D—These are quarter-to-date accumulations of the figures in column B.

Column E—Each figure here is a percentage found by doing the following calculation, where A is the corresponding figure in column A and B is the corresponding figure in column B:

$$\frac{B}{A + B} \times 100$$

Column F—Each figure here is a percentage found by doing the following calculation, where A_4 is the figure obtained by adding up column A for the past four weeks and B_4 is the figure obtained by adding up column B for the past four weeks:

$$\frac{B_4}{A_4 + B_4} \times 100$$

Column G—Each figure here is a percentage found by doing the following calculation, where C is the corresponding figure in column C and D is the corresponding figure in column D:

$$\frac{D}{C + D} \times 100$$

Column H—These figures came from program planning meetings and were entered on the form at the time it was originated in the controller's office.

Column I—The figures in this column were posted by a clerk who took them directly from the Weekly Capital Expenditures Listing.

Column J—These figures came from program planning meetings.

Column K—These figures were derived from a comparison of quarter-to-date and prior year averages. These calculations were done by a clerk who had the necessary information available.

Column L—These figures came from program planning meetings.

Column M—These figures were taken from the Quarterly Earnings Report for Product CDO-1. (See Figure 21.)

Note how well actual performance kept up with goals by comparing columns G and H. Look also at column E. The simple fact that the scrap level of product CDO-1 was receiving management attention drove the traditional scrap level from approximately 70 percent to 60 percent by the middle of the first quarter. Batch numbering and quality assurance controls lowered scrap to 50 percent in the second quarter. The new process control equipment then further reduced scrap to the 10 percent level almost immediately after installation. All ahead of schedule. Scrap levels did rise slightly near year end, as the demand for more product put added pressures on both equipment and personnel. In comparing columns K and L, you can see that actual savings exceeded estimates in each quarter of the year. The controller's estimates of savings, supported in Figure 21, far exceeded those reported on the weekly control reports, because the controller was able to calculate the effect of the CDO-1 project on other products.

Figures 19 and 20 are presented for those who prefer graphical analyses. These figures can be printed out exactly as shown from most computers, with a simple canned program and minimal weekly keypunch input. Figure 19 is a graph of numbers taken from Figure 18. The actual line of Figure 19 is plotted by subtracting column I of Figure 18 from column K on a cumulative, year-to-date basis. The goal line is plotted by subtracting column J from column L in the same manner. In Figure 20 the actual line is plotted from the numbers in column F of Figure 18. The goal line is for the past four weeks; it is derived from numbers not represented in Figure 18.

Figure 21 is the controller's informal quarterly income statement for product CDO-1. Look at some of the things that happened. Even within rigid stipulations regarding standard costs in this firm, the standard cost percentages were reduced in the third and fourth quarters. Cost variances from standard dropped from a traditional 26 percent of sales to almost zero. Sales and

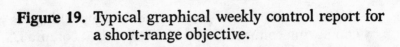

Figure 19. Typical graphical weekly control report for a short-range objective.

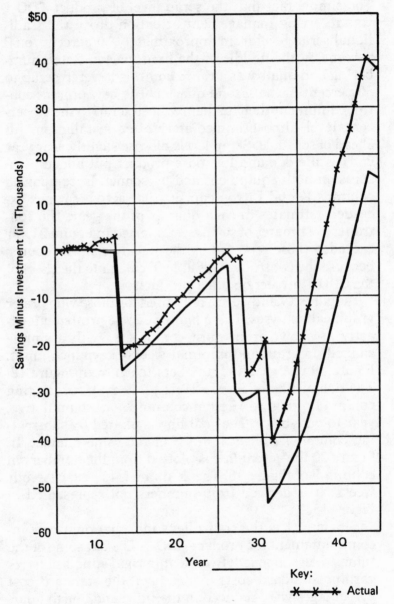

Figure 20. Typical graphical weekly control report for a short-range objective.

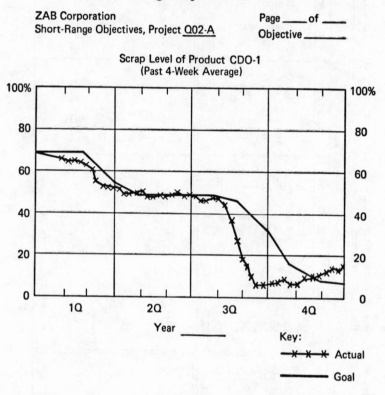

ZAB Corporation
Short-Range Objectives, Project <u>Q02-A</u>

Page ____ of ____
Objective ____

Scrap Level of Product CDO-1
(Past 4-Week Average)

Year ____

Key:
—✕—✕—✕— Actual
————— Goal

Figure 21. Quarterly earnings statement—product CDO-1.

Quarterly Earnings Report for Product CDO-1
Unofficial and Unaudited

Date _____
By _____

| | Last Year | | This Year | | | | | | | | |
| | Average Quarter | | 1st Quarter | | 2nd Quarter | | 3rd Quarter | | 4th Quarter | |
	$000	%	$000	%	$000	%	$000	%	$000	%
Net Sales	208.3	100.0	215.5	100.0	228.9	100.0	225.1	100.0	278.1	100.0
Standard Cost of Goods Sold	135.4	65.0	140.1	65.0	148.8	65.0	144.1	64.0	175.5	63.1
Standard Gross Margin	72.9	35.0	75.4	35.0	80.1	35.0	81.0	36.0	102.6	36.9
Variances from Standard Cost	54.2	26.0	51.9	24.1	40.5	17.7	20.9	9.3	5.0	1.8
Gross Profit	18.7	9.0	23.5	10.9	39.6	17.3	60.1	26.7	97.6	35.1
Sales and General and Administrative Expenses	35.4	17.0	36.6	17.0	38.7	16.9	38.0	16.9	45.9	16.5
Operating Income	(16.7)	(8.0)	(13.1)	(6.1)	0.9	0.4	22.1	9.8	51.7	18.6
Increase in Operating Income over Average Quarter of Last Year			3.6		17.6		38.8		68.4	
Decrease in Cost Variances on Other Products in Departments 3201, 3221, and 3231 Attributed to Reduced Problems with Product CDO-1			4.4		12.5		25.0		36.3	
Net Gain—Objective Q02			8.0		30.1		63.8		104.7	

general and administrative costs did not drop as much as anticipated, in that they included distribution costs and sales increases were being realized from the more distant markets. A major savings was effected in the processing of other products. In this case, product CDO-1 historically represented only about 6 percent of corporate sales. But by eliminating myriad frustrations and problems related to the processing of CDO-1, overall cost variances diminished significantly throughout the plant. With only slightly more than 50 percent of the sales potential of the product realized by the fourth quarter, that product improvement was already responsible for a net gain in operating income of over $100,000 a quarter.

For the short-range objectives program, it is strongly recommended that a report similar to that shown in Figure 18 be prepared for each objective. A weekly package of the reports should then be circulated confidentially to the key personnel involved. Such a practice aids in keeping the program on the front burner and demonstrates once more the strength of the turnaround manager's commitment to the turnaround program.

If corporate policy permits open knowledge of the information, and if acceptable conference room facilities are available, additional mileage can be gained by exhibiting overall progress, as well as progress by function, on large wall graphs.

Finally, as mentioned earlier, the proof of the pudding is the monthly or, more probably, the quarterly income statement. The short-range objectives program should be considered a failure until progress becomes evident on that income statement.

At the time of adjournment of the planning session, none of these objectives should be considered as being cast in concrete. All phases of management are dynamic, not static. Just as the project discussed in this chapter was modified to include expensive new equipment, most projects should be improved, in one way or another, as they progress.

Recognition

With one exception, this is not the time to tie individual monetary rewards directly to program accomplishment. Immediate gains are too easily achieved, and there are a number of other, more effective means of recognizing people for their contributions. Few authorities on incentive compensation would recommend the implementation of any sort of incentive plan by a business whose foundation is so shaky that a major turnaround is required in order for the business to survive. That would be akin to paying a premium for showing up at work.

The one exception might exist in an organization with a tradition of granting interim salary increases for cases of extraordinary performance. But mere achievement of any of the established goals in the short-range program should not be considered extraordinary. As the program gains momentum and enthusiasm builds, however, it is not uncommon for a participant to originate a simple action that results in an unexpected annual savings of $250,000 or more. In such cases, an interim salary increase, which does not upset the overall salary structure, might be appropriate.

Occasional luncheon meetings of the staff at a nice restaurant—with no business conversation—often promote teamwork. Staff members' birthdays are good excuses for such gatherings.

But the good old standard forms of recognition still work wonders and are absolutely necessary in this situation. Individual recognition heads the list. The turnaround manager should always be prepared to meaningfully compliment each employee upon their meeting. A special call to the office, the bulletin board, and the in-house newsletter each offer opportunities for sincere compliments. How did you feel when the boss paid you a meaningful compliment? Individual recognition also has another form, criticism. Subordinates expect it, just as our children do. To be most effective, complimentary recognition must be coupled with private critical recognition. Sincerity becomes diluted without it.

Job understanding is another form of worthwhile recognition. Like the stonemason who thought of himself not as a bricklayer but as a cathedral builder, people appreciate their own contributions more and, as a result, perform better, as their understanding of their role in the overall scheme of things increases. Don't bypass an opportunity to let all subordinates know how their individual efforts contribute to the whole.

A third effective form of recognition is job enlargement. At this point in the turnaround process, job enlargement in the form of promotion would be premature for much the same reasons as those advanced against salary increases. But there are other ways to achieve a similar end. An extracurricular assignment, for example. To the human relations manager, "Tim, I've been reading quite a bit about on-site child care centers lately. Would you look into it and let me know if it would work for us?" Or a request to a subordinate who enjoys the outside limelight to represent you and the company at an important affair. Or to a subordinate in passing, "A small matter has come up that requires my attention, and I was wondering if you would mind taking care of it for me?"

Finally, there are the behavior patterns and individual wants and needs, that surfaced in Chapter 5. These should be utilized throughout the turnaround program in rewarding and developing key personnel.

As your short-range projects progress successfully, it is time to begin preparing for the longer-range program outlined in Chapter 13. But while doing this, keep the short-range program moving ahead with involvement, control, and recognition.

12
Implement Budget Policies and Programs

BUDGETING is another basic managment tool that is commonly missing from, or misused by, companies in need of a turnaround. In many cases, where a knowledgeable bird's-eye view of a failing business indicates poor financial management to be the prime cause, the professional worm's-eye picture will show that most of the problems could have been avoided merely by the application of sound basic budgeting practices.

Two examples come to mind. The first involves a nonprofit service organization in a rapidly growing suburban area. Local population had doubled each decade during the preceding 50 years, while the nonprofit organization had grown only 10 percent in the preceding 20 years, and was having a continuing problem meeting its routine expenses. An annual budget was perfunctorily prepared each year by an executive committee, approved at the annual meeting, and promptly filed under F for "forgotten." Accurate monthly financial statements were faithfully issued by the Accounting Department with no concern or reference to the established budget. In fact, the budget and financial reports were prepared in two different formats that could not be compared. A few simple changes—(1) agreement on a single format for budgeting and financial reporting, (2) an annual budget providing for organization growth at least equal to the anticipated population growth of the area served, and (3) financial reporting comparing actual to budgeted results on monthly and year-to-date bases—drew the leaders of that organization together to a shared purpose that led to the launching of a period of rapid and successful growth.

The second example involved a $300 million division of a major corporation with an extremely large and expensive corporate headquarters operation. Some years earlier, when the corporate staff was only skeletal, a budgeting procedure had been initiated. It included a monthly corporate service fee charged to the general and administrative expenses of each division based on the budgeted current assets of that division. The division in question was by far the largest in the corporation and thus bore the lion's share of the corporate charge. However, being reasonably self-sufficient, it utilized the smallest portion of corporate services. Corporate services were devoted primarily to acquisitions and assistance to fledgling divisions.

To make matters worse, the corporate staff, which played a key role in budgeting for the newer and smaller divisions, was given increasing authority to modify budgets of the larger, more senior entities. As a result, a company once proud and profitable became demoralized by a rapidly growing budget and expense burden (over which it had no control), which forced it below the break-even line. Managers in that division began each year with feelings of frustration because of a budget pill too large to swallow. Finally, someone got the bright idea of establishing the corporate headquarters as a profit center, compelled to operate at a budget of no more than 2 percent of the total sales of its divisions. Each division was then budgeted and billed 1 percent of its monthly sales, plus a fee for any special corporate services, which it reported below the operating income line. This one change enabled the division in question to once again budget and report a respectable profit. The enthusiasm that resulted helped considerably in transforming a long-dormant company into a vibrantly expanding business.

Thus, before beginning the strategic long-range

planning of your turnaround, it is important to make certain that your budgeting practices are sound and sufficiently flexible to be incorporated with your plans. Your accounting reports must be designed to reflect actual turnaround progress, and your budgeting practices must be designed to reflect turnaround goals in that same format.

Budget Requirements

This chapter is devoted to a brief discussion of four types of budgets recommended for use in the turnaround program.

1. The personnel staffing budget.
2. The income and expense budget.
3. The capital expenditures budget.
4. The cash flow budget.

All may employ extremely sophisticated techniques, but here, again, a simple and basic approach is recommended, at least until the business becomes untangled from its own underwear. Sophistication will enter the scene with strategic long-range planning. However, our current objective continues to be to establish a sturdy foundation with all necessary built-in service connections, on which to build our architectural masterpiece.

The four types of budgets have certain common requirements:

1. They all must accurately reflect established corporate objectives. They must be a part of the formal turnaround program. Many people would be surprised at how often this is not the case. For example, an income and expense budget for the forthcoming year is constructed within the Finance function by applying logical X percent, Y percent, and Z percent adjustments to the performance of the prior year, and it is officially approved. The same company also has an approved set of turnaround goals for the ensuing year that bear little or no relationship to the budgeted percentages. Two goals, two different road maps, two masters—it doesn't work.

Turnaround goals must be incorporated in the budget so that all are working toward a single end.

2. Budgets must be flexible, so that they may be changed as plans change. They must be dynamic, just as the business to which they apply is dynamic. This does not mean that budgets should be susceptible to daily change. It is recommended that they be established for a year in advance and fixed for the quarter immediately ahead. Then, on a quarterly basis, the budgets for succeeding quarters should be modified by adjusting the budgets for the remaining three quarters, adding a new fourth quarter, and making a locked-in commitment to the budget as then modified for the quarter just ahead.

Again, in all cases, the budget modifications should coincide with adjustments made in the business plan.

3. Budgets should be realistic but difficult to attain. They are not meant to be philanthropic, so that attainment will provide the same sense of accomplishment that one gets from dropping a wad of paper into a wastebasket while standing directly above it. Nor are budgets meant to be so powerful that attainment becomes as difficult as hitting that wastebasket from the far corner of the room. Budgets are meant to be competitive, requiring a reasonable degree of skill to hit the basket placed a reasonable distance away. Budgeted goals should be set so that they cannot be reached merely by adequate management. They should have about a 90 percent chance of being attained by good management, and a 90 percent chance of being exceeded by excellent management. And the goals for each succeeding budget period should be slightly more difficult to reach than those of the last period.

Budget attainment should foster an enthusiastic sense of accomplishment and the desire to shoot at a more difficult target.

4. Budget preparation and reporting should in-

clude considerable involvement of all managerial personnel. Preparation should grow from the bottom up. It should not be imposed from the top down.

Picture this discourse between the manager in a placement agency and one of her employees. "Shirley, your goal for the next quarter is four placements a week." "But how can I do that? You know that everyone is laying off and no one is hiring." "Don't ask me; those are the boss's orders."

Businesses are loaded with Shirleys, professional people who have no voice in setting their goals and receive little advice from above on how they are expected to achieve unrealistic objectives that are imposed on them.

We know that people perform best to goals that they participate in establishing. And not only do the chances of attainment increase through such participation, but the goals themselves are usually set at a higher level.

It is likely that had Shirley and her coworkers in the placement agency been called in by the manager to discuss quarterly goals, they would have jointly produced the creative thinking necessary to meet the boss's preconceived objective of four placements per person per week.

Upper-level managers must initiate the budgeting process by forecasting the general activity parameters, sales, new orders, and so forth, and then build a budget at the lowest level of management, modifying items as needed to meet the plan, as the budget works its way up to final approval. Permit the front-line managers to estimate the staffing and expenses they need to meet budgeted activity levels. Even though many of these estimates may require modification, these managers will strive harder to meet the budget.

Then, after the budget is formally adopted, regularly inform all managers of their actual performance to it.

The best-managed manufacturing operation I know owes a good deal of its success to an extremely high degree of budget involvement. First-line supervisors participate in establishing the direct labor budgets for their departments, following the cardinal rule that the budgeted hours per unit of production must always be less than those budgeted for the prior quarter. All supervisors are then required to calculate their individual department's actual direct labor performance daily, report it at a 9:30 A.M. supervisors' meeting the following morning, and explain any discrepancies to budget. Most supervisors enlist the help of office clerks, with the promise of a small Christmas gift, to make the daily calculation from time cards delivered to them by the supervisor. Thus the office, too, is brought into this game of "Beat the daily labor budget." That company continues to grow, leading its industry in profit percentage.

5. The standard acorns of understanding and commitment merit being noted here as well. For budgets to be effective, all involved must understand their purpose, their content, and their sanctity and must be fully committed to their attainment. And understanding must precede commitment, because people can't commit to doing something they don't fully understand.

In the area of understanding, the budget is usually looked on as a table of numerical values. It should be more than that, in that the supporting documents used in its construction should note how the improved numbers are expected to be attained.

"This year's sales will be about $50 million. Let's budget a 20 percent increase, $60 million, for next year." That type of budgeting, all too common among companies in trouble, is meaningless without a valid plan for achieving the sales increase.

6. All reports of actual performance should include a comparison with the corresponding budget. What was done has little significance until it is compared with what could and should have been done in the same time frame. "Our sales were $3,000,000 last month." "Does that mean I should hug you or fire you?"

7. The budget should be in sufficient detail to be

meaningful, but not in so much detail as to be burdensome. The amount of detail in budgeting and reporting should increase with each lower level of the organization.

Some companies seem to restrict the number of line items they budget and report on the premise that every human being has a capacity to digest only so many numbers. A sounder approach would be to budget and report all line items that either are immediately significant to the recipient or might be of value to that person as a reference.

Take a staffing budget as an example. One number, total employees, would be insufficient for any level of management. The president might be satisfied with three categories: direct labor, factory indirect, and all other. The factory supervisor might need a far more detailed breakdown, in a format that could be used for such purposes as planning ways in which jobs might be combined.

The Sales Forecast

The first step in preparing all budgets is the development and adoption of a sales forecast for the period in question. That forecast must incorporate all of the short- and long-range planning and MWO objectives, or these objectives should be changed to conform to the forecast that is prepared. Such change of objectives, however, should be considered in only the most extreme circumstances. Also, the forecast should be in the degree of detail required to adequately budget the other business functions. For example, sales forecasts by product line and geographical area may be needed to support production planning, distribution, and financial budgets.

The development work done in the planning processes should have been sufficient to provide reasonably accurate sales forecasts, at least for the next quarter. In some cases, the validation and use of lead indicators, such as the Dodge Reports for a construction-related business, may be very helpful in forecasting. However, a knowledge of the industry involved, including key competitors, and of general economic predictions, is usually sufficient for the company involved in a turn-around.

Frequently, a sound forecast will require several special considerations for a handful of products and/or geographical areas.

Naturally, as the accuracy of the forecast increases, the cost of operations for the period forecasted tends to decrease. For example, if the sales forecast were perfect, the precise needs of each department would be known in advance. As a result, there should be no personnel or inventory overages or shortages.

Production people frequently make better sales forecasters than do sales personnel. Apparently their estimates are taken from a broader base and are less influenced by new orders received in the past week or by the last conversation with a customer.

With today's electronic sophistication, much can be done to increase the degree of accuracy in the sales forecast. Econometric and economic models, with known levels of risk or error, may be developed and used in the process.

These models and indicators can be compared with the feedback of actual sales results. Available programming techniques permit the development of a history of these comparisons so that the programs become more and more fine-tuned and the sales forecasts automatically are self-improving.

A very simple and effective forecasting control tool might be a comparison of actual sales for a period with sales forecast by individual key staff members. This can result in a consensus forecast formula, with the lowest, quantified level of risk.

As soon as the sales forecast has been agreed on, it

should be released to the resource planners for their use and to the accounting group for explosion into the income and expense budget.

The Personnel Staffing Budget

All managers should be involved in budgeting the staffing needs for their particular departments.

The quarterly staffing budget is initiated by Accounting, where a budget work sheet is prepared for each department. Figure 22 is an example of a work sheet that accounting personnel have prepared for a shipping department. The work sheet lists each person in the department by name and position. On the same line is that person's current hourly rate (interpolated for salaried personnel). Budgeted and actual staffing levels for the prior two quarters are shown in the four columns following the Position column. Note that these columns allow comparison of budgeted and actual numbers of employees; for example, for the position of Shipper II, two positions had been budgeted, but only one was actually filled in Q-2. That would also account for the fact that in Q-2, overtime pay was much more than anticipated. The work sheet also shows budgeted and actual sales for the prior two quarters and forecast sales for the next four quarters. These can be found in the bottom half of the chart.

After the Accounting Department has filled out the work sheet up to this point, it is distributed to the appropriate heads of the major functions of the business. The functional heads are responsible for noting the following items (which can be found on Figure 23, a completed staffing budget):

1. Anticipated staffing changes, in the Position column, and related pay scales, in the columns for budget for the next four quarters.

2. Planned merit pay increases in the columns for budget for the next four quarters. Note that the two supervisors, who are salaried personnel, are budgeted to receive merit increases. In this company salaried employees are more likely to be budgeted for individual merit increases than are hourly employees. Note also that the automatic pay increases for both salaried and hourly workers are described under budgeted general wage increases and are reflected in the budgeted payroll adjustment amount for the next four quarters.

3. Estimated overtime hours for each of the succeeding four quarters.

4. Initialed approval of these additional entries, on the right-hand side of the work sheet.

The functional executives may either delegate the responsibility for filling out these items to the individual department heads reporting to them or work with them in completing it.

The work sheets are then forwarded to the next higher level of management for initialed approval or rejection. Any rejections during the approval process should, of course, be discussed with the initiating manager.

The approved forms are then forwarded to the Budget Department for completion. As Figure 23 shows, budget personnel record any anticipated general wage increases not already accounted for and complete the arithmetic extensions, thus finalizing the budgets.

The completed staffing budget is then forwarded to the Personnel Department, as an authorized limitation on hiring during the period covered by the budget. Note that the budget is not an authority to hire. Hiring requires a properly authorized employment requisition. However, the budget does advise the human resources manager that any employment requisition that would increase any department's staff beyond that budgeted must bear your initials as the turnaround manager.

(text continues on page 176)

Figure 22. Staffing budget as issued by Accounting to each manager.

CONFIDENTIAL   Shipping   **Payroll and Staffing Budget**   Qtr _____ 19 _____

Department _____

| Department | S or H* | Name | Position | Hourly Rate: A = Actual   B = Budget | | | | | | | | | Approved by |
				B Q-2	A Q-2	B Q-1	A Q-1	A Now	B Q+1	B Q+2	B Q+3	B Q+4	
1	S	A. Shulze	Gen'l Supervisor	1	1	1	1	14.36					
2	S	H. Vigorus	Supervisor	2	2	2	2	10.98					
3	S	P. Darno	Supervisor					11.28					
4	H	L. Van Rae	Clerk	1	1	1	1	6.36					
5	H	R. Smith	Shipper I	2	2	2	2	8.62					
6	H	C. Schwartz	Shipper I					8.62					
7	H	H. Fresca	Shipper II	2	1	1	1	6.97					
8	H	R. Michel	Handler	4	4	4	4	6.36					
9	H	C. Reichen	Handler					6.36					
10	H	R. Johns	Handler					6.36					
11	H	K. Home	Handler					6.36					
12	H	J. Kerse	Loader	5	5	6	6	5.73					
13	H	W. Winger	Loader					5.73					
14	H	F. Hesselman	Loader					5.73					
15	H	D. McKeon	Loader					5.73					
16	H	L. Missback	Loader					5.73					
17	H	P. Prete	Loader					5.58					
18													
19													
20													
21													
22													
23													
24													

	B Q-2	A Q-2	B Q-1	A Q-1	A Now	B Q+1	B Q+2	B Q+3	B Q+4	Approved by
					Hourly Rate: A = Actual B = Budget					
Sales ($000)	1,929	1,924	2,195	2,237		3,163	3,572	4,070	4,738	
Total number of people	17	16	17	17	17					
Straight-time hourly payroll										
Straight-time weekly payroll										
Straight-time quarterly payroll										
Overtime hours for quarter	455	1,248	455	416						
Pay for quarter (1½ time—hourly only)										
Total payroll at above rates										
Budgeted general wage increases										
Payroll adjustment amount										
Total payroll										
Justification for recommended changes:										

* Key: S=Salaried H=Hourly

Figure 23. Completed staffing budget.

Department _____ Shipping   Payroll and Staffing Budget

Hourly Rate: A=Actual   B=Budget

#	S or H*	Name	Position	B Q-2	A Q-2	B Q-1	A Q-1	A Now	B Q+1	B Q+2	B Q+3	B Q+4	Approved by
1	S	A. Shulze	Gen'l Supervisor	1	1	1	1	14.36					LMP RJM
2	S	H. Vigorus	Supervisor	2	2	2	2	10.98	11.19	11.52	11.52	11.52	AS LMP RJM
3	S	P. Darno	Supervisor					11.28	11.37	11.52	11.52	11.52	AS LMP RJM
4	H	L. Van Rae	Clerk	1	1	1	1	6.36					AS LMP RJM
5	H	R. Smith	Shipper I	2	2	2	2	8.62					AS LMP RJM
6	H	C. Schwartz	Shipper I					8.62					AS LMP RJM
7	H	H. Fresca	Shipper II	2	1	1	1	6.97					AS LMP RJM
8	H	R. Michel	Handler	4	4	4	4	6.36					AS LMP RJM
9	H	C. Reichen	Handler					6.36					AS LMP RJM
10	H	R. Johns	Handler					6.36					AS LMP RJM
11	H	K. Home	Handler					6.36					AS LMP RJM
12	H	J. Kerse	Loader	5	5	6	6	5.73					AS LMP RJM
13	H	W. Winger	Loader					5.73					AS LMP RJM
14	H	F. Hesselman	Loader					5.73					AS LMP RJM
15	H	D. McKeon	Loader					5.73					AS LMP RJM
16	H	L. Missback	Loader					5.73					AS LMP RJM
17	H	P. Prete	Loader					5.58	5.73	5.58	5.73	5.73	AS LMP RJM
18	H		Loader								6.21	6.36	AS LMP RJM
19	H		Handler										AS LMP RJM
20	H		Loader								5.58	5.73	AS LMP RJM
21	H		Loader										AS LMP RJM
22	H		Clerk								5.58	5.73	AS LMP RJM
23	H		Loader									5.58	AS LMP RJM
24	H		Shipper II									6.82	AS LMP RJM

Hourly Rate: A = Actual B = Budget

	B Q-2	A Q-2	B Q-1	A Q-1	A Now	B Q+1	B Q+2	B Q+3	B Q+4	Approved by
Sales ($000)	1,929	1,924	2,195	2,237		3,163	3,572	4,070	4,738	
Total number of people	17	16	17	17	17	17	18	22	24	
Straight-time hourly payroll					126.86	127.31	133.37	156.47	169.47	
Straight-time weekly payroll						5,092	5,335	6,259	6,779	
Straight-time quarterly payroll						66,201	69,352	81,364	88,124	
Overtime hours for quarter	455	1,248	455	416		364	390	618	683	AS LM? RUM
Pay for quarter (1½ time—hourly only)						3,525	3,743	5,809	6,443	
Total payroll at above rates						69,726	73,095	87,173	94,567	
Budgeted general wage increases	9% hourly on 1/1; 10% salaried non-exempt on 2/1; 10% salaried exempt on 3/1									
Payroll adjustment amount						5,208	6,806	8,102	8,767	
Total payroll						74,934	79,901	95,275	103,334	
Justification for recommended changes:	Added Volume									

* Key: S = Salaried H = Hourly

The Income and Expense Budget

Here, again, the guidelines set forth for all budgets at the beginning of this chapter apply.

The suggested procedure is very much the same as that for staffing budgets.

The individual in charge of budget preparation should first check with you and with the executive in charge of each function to determine where more or less budget detail is needed by any of them. To repeat, the degree of detail should be the minimum necessary to provide meaningful information and the capacity to measure progress toward planned goals.

Once this has been decided, the budget chief should draw up the work sheets, including the budgeted sales, payroll costs, and obligatory fixed charges for the budget period. Four columns should be drawn in order to show related actual and budgeted costs for the two prior quarters.

After allowing a few days for the heads of the functions to discuss the budget for their respective areas with subordinates, the budget chief should meet with each functional head. The Accounting Department can then begin working on the arithmetic required to put the income and expense budget into complete detailed and summary form. All questionable items should be brought to the attention of, and approved by, the chief executive, prior to their incorporation in the summary calculations.

One final comment on income and expense budgets. They can be given too much, as well as too little, consideration. Fifth decimal place estimates of items that cannot be controlled in less than whole units is a common mistake. And most budgeters have discovered by experience that a third, fourth, and fifth rehash of individual line items have very little effect on the total budget of any given department.

The Capital Expenditures Budget

A few slightly different ground rules are usually followed with respect to the capital budget. For example, the period budgeted is frequently longer. A time frame of two to five years might be required to include anticipated building and acquisition projects.

An adequate procedure is for the budget chief to distribute a copy of the capital budget for the prior quarter to the head of each function, updated to include actual capital expenditure activity. With that should go a request to revise and update it, adding an additional quarter, with all known and anticipated needs. Many of these needs will have already been agreed upon at prior company planning sessions. The recipient discusses the budget with subordinates and records his or her recommendations, noting the item, the reason for needing it, and its estimated cost in terms of when payment demands are anticipated. The budget work sheet is then forwarded to you for editing and approval. It is then passed on to the budget chief for the purpose of consolidation.

This budget must also provide for unforeseen emergencies such as major equipment failure or building repairs, especially in later quarters. Therefore, it should include a contingency line to cover such events. This contingency provision is best set either as a fixed dollar amount or as a percentage of the total dollars budgeted for known items. It should be nominal for the near future, but it should increase with succeeding time periods, just as do the unknowns.

Once again, the capital budget must not be used as an authorization to make any capital expenditures. Each such expenditure must be authorized only by an appropriately approved capital expenditure request form, on which the anticipated return on investment has been adequately developed and presented.

The Cash Flow Budget

The Accounting Department can generate a weekly forecast of the sources and application of cash directly from the income and expense and capital budgets.

This cash flow budget should include recommendations for sources of funds in periods when cash is projected to be insufficient to meet the needs of the business. It should also note recommendations for application of surplus idle money.

Putting It Together

You should discuss the completed budgets with your subordinate finance head(s) and then approve them as a package.

This step frequently demands some massaging in order to arrive at a budget that reflects preplanned goals. Budgets, especially when constructed from the bottom up in an organization, sometimes fail to reflect the profit objectives of the firm. Such cases demand that you make difficult pruning decisions. However, before any budgeted item is changed, the person responsible for the function affected should be consulted and made aware of the reasoning behind the proposed change.

The Contingency Plan

Along with each budget package, every good turnaround executive will have a formal, flexible contingency plan filed close at hand.

This plan will note specific courses of action to be taken, and to be taken seriously, for each 10 percent increment by which actual sales fall short of budget and the permissible maximum delay between shortfall and corrective action.

A contingency plan might, for example, include your answers to the following questions: What will you do if an unexpected decline in economic conditions results in sales that fall 10 percent short of budget? What jobs will you eliminate or combine? Which planned expenditures will you postpone? How long will you weather decreased sales before taking action? You should develop and privately record your tentative answers to such questions before budgets are released.

13
Develop
and Implement a
Long-Range
Strategic Plan

NOW you are about to take the one turnaround step that, far more than any other, separates the winners from the losers.

It is true that any business is only as good as its people. It is often true that the business that offers its customers the best value/price ratio will be the most successful. The amount spent on, and effectiveness of, advertising seems to be the key to success for many consumer products. Most executives would argue that a plan is no good without strong follow-up action to support it.

All these are individual strategies included in a typical program of strategic planning. The odds are slight that you will discover which combination of individual strategies will work well for your company until you have gone through the laborious exercise of corporate-wide strategic planning.

You will discover that the velocity, amplitude, and life span of your turnaround will depend more on the results of your strategic planning effort than on anything else. To put this point another way, the other chapters of this book are devoted to effective use of bandaids, cough syrup, and penicillin shots. This chapter recommends a healthy business life style that has been proven to be most effective in lengthening corporate life spans.

Many organizations have found the strategic planning activity itself to be more beneficial than the plan they adopted. The ignition of creativity; the dependence on integrated teamwork; the information unearthed about customers and competitors, internal and external resources, and organizational relations; and an education in the techniques surrounding selection and implementation of alternative strategies could in the long run pay greater dividends than the choice of any one strategy.

Because strategic planning is an essential part of the turnaround process, I feel that it must be addressed in this book. However, because it demands an exhaustive treatment in order for its implementation to be reasonably successful, the reader should be alerted that only the tip of an iceberg is being shown here.

Many excellent texts on strategic planning have been published, some devoted to the overall theme and others covering only one or two of the many techniques involved. Before entering the strategic planning segment of the turnaround program, you should definitely update your reading on the subject. For this, I strongly recommend two books by William E. Rothschild: *Putting It All Together* (New York: AMACOM, 1976) and *Strategic Alternatives* (New York: AMACOM, 1979).

Even more important is the need for preliminary training of all key personnel who will be involved in the planning process. Here, too, a number of excellent alternatives are available. For such training, I prefer to enroll my immediate subordinates as a unit in a strategic planning seminar with a workshop format. There they can actually begin development of the company's strategic plan by applying real situations as they climb the learning tree of creative business strategy. In addition, they will be subjected to the unifying force of learning the same techniques from the same people at the same time.

You must make a choice between in-house and public seminars. The first offers the advantage of exclusivity—all discussion will center on your own organization. The second offers the advantage of more cross-pollination, building ideas for your company on thoughts advanced from other types of businesses. I prefer that turnaround managers attend both, first a general seminar and then a seminar with their staffs, exclusively tailored to their special situations.

The time period required to develop the long-range strategic plan will vary considerably, depending on the size and type of business as well as on the amount of prerequisite information already available. Small to medium-size organizations, with a good data bank of information about their industry, customers, and competitors, might complete the task in less than 90 days. Larger companies, requiring considerable research in order to obtain sufficient basic knowledge of their marketplace, may require a much longer period for plan development.

There seem to be as many formats for strategic business plans as there are companies that have them. Also, definitions of terms and elements included in those plans vary widely. The strategic plan for one company may be an idea in the mind of the president that remains constant or changes daily and is often heard but seldom reduced to writing. This form of strategic planning leads to the need for a turnaround more often than to the accomplishment of one. Other companies approach the opposite extreme, with written strategic plans several hundred pages long, incorporating a mission statement, a list of strategies, a further delineation of those strategies into specific objectives, a breakdown of objectives into the tasks necessary to attain them, and a host of supportive exhibits, each element having been arrived at by means of state-of-the-art, sophisticated, analytical processes. This degree of comprehensiveness is equally unproductive for a company in the turnaround mode.

To turn around, the company must know where it is, decide where it wants to go (objectives), and plan an efficient route for getting there (strategies). But time is of the essence, and the first attempt at any strategic planning is usually most effective when aimed at reaching not-too-distant destinations by the most direct and economical routes. Coincidentally, this usually dovetails with turnaround requirements, a few basic improvements in several functions of the business.

Sophistication in the planning process will grow naturally with the experience of those participating in it and with company needs that develop after the turnaround is accomplished. But during the first attempt, it is imperative that the levels of comprehensiveness and sophistication remain well within the digestion limits of participants. Otherwise, the plan just won't work.

In a turnaround situation, an effective strategic plan should include a mission statement and an organized listing of objectives (where you want to go) and strategies (how you want to get there); it should cover at least the next three, and preferably the next five, years; and it should include the documents needed to adequately support the chosen strategies. Its implementation should include scheduled task lists to provide for attainment of each stated strategy and a series of regular control reports designed both to monitor performance to plan and to keep the program on track.

The plan should become the corporate bible, a constant source of reference for the managers involved. The control reports will provide a regular short-interval means of reference and symptomatic revelations of the need for minor tuneups. It is suggested that major tuneups be made annually or as major new influences arise, whichever comes first. Complete overhauls should be scheduled every two years.

The Components of the Strategic Plan

Before discussing plan preparation and implementation, let me expand a bit on the definition of each of the four elements to be included:

1. *Mission statement.*The strategic plan should begin

with a statement of mission, influenced primarily by the customers or clients to be served and reflecting the philosophies of the owners and officers of the business.

The following is an example of a simple, but adequate, mission statement.

> Manufacture and market a broad line of products that satisfy the needs of all manufacturing jewelers in the continental United States. Maintain a minimum return of 20 percent on assets employed and a real annual growth rate of 15 percent. Utilize existing strengths of providing products not readily available from other sources, introducing innovative and improved products, and offering shorter lead times than competitors.

The mission statement then becomes the focal point for each objective to be included in the plan. At the outset, the mission statement is intended to serve as a guide for the development of objectives and strategies. As these are developed and tested, they may, in turn, generate a modification, extension, or constriction of the initial mission statement.

2. *List of objectives*. Objectives are the specific goals necessary to accomplish a stated mission. Therefore, your long-range strategic plan should contain as many objectives as are required to achieve its mission. Objectives should also be grouped together in some logical form. A commonly used grouping, with an example of an objective for each, is:

> *Marketing objectives*. Increase sales in New England states from $2 million to $10 million per year, over next five years.
>
> *Financial resource objectives*. Finance growth from internally generated cash.
>
> *Physical resource objectives*. Maintain utilization of plant facilities at 85 to 90 percent of capacity throughout plan period.
>
> *Human resource objectives*. Reduce relative salaried payroll from 10 to 9 percent of sales over plan period.

In cases where a single objective fits into several groups, it should be included in the group to which it seems most logically attached. Precision in grouping of objectives is not critical to the success of the plan.

3. *List of strategies.* Objectives, in turn, lead to the establishment of strategies and the policy and practice statements needed to effect them. Take the objective of a real growth rate of 15 percent per year. That statement must be expanded significantly in order to produce an acceptable degree of confidence in a company's ability to achieve the objective. An integrated series of specific supportive strategies must be established. In addition, policy statements, such as one defining authority in deciding on new products, may be in order. And some companies might find it advantageous to formally outline the procedure to be followed in bringing a new product on stream.

These strategies must be included as part of the formal strategic plan. Having an objective without strategies is about as hopeless a situation as planning to buy a house on the moon in the next few months.

Then, to assure that the selected strategies are implemented, they must be broken down into specific goals, such as the MWOs expressed in Chapter 10.

4. *Supportive exhibits.* The fourth ingredient of a long-range strategic plan is the supportive exhibits. These should include all tabular and graphical data necessary to adequately clarify the text, showing where the company is now and where it will be at various milestones along the planned strategic route. Analyses of competition, past and projected sales, and current and projected financial reports are typical of such exhibits.

Strategic Plan Preparation

Strategic plan preparation requires a strong combination of creative thinking and painstaking work.

Let's examine the basic preparatory work required:

Step 1. *Where are we now?* By answering a series of appropriate questions, you can construct a formidable base from which to launch your strategic plan. Many of these questions have already been answered in your financial inventory, functional audit, and other programs discussed earlier in this book. Those answers need only be restructured into the strategic planning format of:

Marketing

Financial resources

Physical resources

Human resources

But a certain amount of additional effort will be needed to supply the answers to some of the questions I have included at the end of this step. To do this, it is recommended that all functional heads be given a list of the questions and asked to apply the questions to their respective functions and answer on that basis.

Some group discussion should then take place to arrive at consensus answers that are clear and comprehensive.

Four sets of answers, one for each planning category, must be supplied for each of these five questions:

1. What are our greatest strengths, opportunities, and problems in this area? How can we exploit the strengths and opportunities and resolve the problems?
2. What are our current and recent objectives in this area? Which have been easiest and which most difficult to achieve? Why?
3. What are our current and recent strategies in this area? Which have succeeded and which have failed? Why?
4. What external factors apply to this area—political, governmental, environmental, and so forth? What have been the trends of their impact? What can their impact be expected to be in the next five years?

5. Are there any cross-conflicts between current objectives and strategies? Where? How serious are they?

In addition, there are questions that apply individually to each of the four categories:

Marketing

6. What have been the sales and profitability of each of our products/services over the past ten years? What have been their growth rates?
7. What is the market definition, in terms of customers and geography, for each of our products or services?
8. For each product and service, how do we compare with competitors in market share? Quality? Price? Competitive strengths and weaknesses?
9. What has been our pricing policy? How effective is it?
10. What is the quality level of our products and services? How do major customers perceive our company and its products and services?

Financial Resources

11. At what level have key financial indicators been for each of the past five years? What have been the trends of these indicators? How do they compare to industry averages and to averages reported by competitors? (Key financial indicators are discussed in Chapter 3).
12. What have been the sources for required funds over the past five years? How much has come from each source? How much more capital is available from these sources? What other possible sources are there?

Physical Resources

13. What are our major, or critical, fixed assets? At what capacity are they currently utilized? How

much time before they must be replaced because of obsolescence or condition? What are they worth in book value, market value, replacement cost?

14. What are our major raw materials? What will be their availability and price in future years? What, if any, substitutes are viable?

15. What will be the impact of technology on our current physical resources of fixed assets, materials, and information management techniques?

Human Resources

16. How is the organization structured? How should it be structured in order to reach maximum return?

17. At what level are morale, understanding, commitment, working conditions, and communications?

18. Where is the current labor market, and in which direction is it moving? Are there, or will there be, any problems in acquiring and retaining key personnel at the present pay scale? If the company is organized, what is the current condition of union relations? When does the union contract expire?

These questions usually represent only a minor percentage of those addressed in most strategic planning programs. You may wish to add a few questions to improve the focus on your particular business. However, they should be sufficient to establish the base needed for a turnaround. Sophistication can be added as the business improves and as the staff acquires more exposure to strategic planning.

It is most important that these questions, alternate answers, and consensus answers be transcribed in a professional style. Handwritten sheets or typewritten summaries are not acceptable. The information should be presented on forms and graphs designed to project clarity and understanding as well as professional consideration and judgment.

Such presentation will enhance the success of a strategic plan in two ways. First, those who are about to make decisions on where to go and how to get there will have a much clearer picture of where they are starting from. They will also have a much better multidirectional view of the terrain ahead.

Second, a first-class presentation will add much to the confidence level of the planners, as well as to those who must approve the final strategic plan. As they refer back to your assessment of current conditions, if it is professionally documented, the planners will do their planning with the assurance that they have started from a very strong home base.

People who know their starting point, the means of available transportation, and the surrounding terrain and who possess confidence in their own ability to arrive at any given destination usually will be successful in getting there.

Step 2. *Where do we want to go?* Three steps are necessary in establishing long-range company objectives. As in the assessment just completed, these steps must be taken skillfully and carefully. Here, too, the results should be presented as professionally as can possibly be done with available resources.

Start by reviewing the present and anticipated impacts of external factors. As accurately as possible, list all factors that will, or might, pose a threat or provide an opportunity for your business. Quantify your estimates in terms of effect on sales and/or pretax earnings. Qualify the level of risk for each effect as either high, medium, or low.

Next, under each of the four planning categories, list all the future results you would like to achieve in that area. These are your preliminary objectives. Many may be the same as those you already have established.

To complete this portion of the process, you and your

staff should evaluate your listed objectives in the sequence that follows:

1. Check for cross-conflicts among objectives and resolve them. For example, a marketing objective that demands doubling plant and equipment might be in conflict with resource objectives that indicate the lack of funds, land, or prospective employees. This task may be delegated to one or two qualified persons.
2. Check objectives against your risk evaluation of external factors. Note the possible impact of each beside the particular objective. This task, too, may be delegated.
3. Set a numerical priority on each objective. There are many sophisticated means available for numerically establishing priorities, but they are seldom needed in a turnaround situation. An easy yet effective way is to rate each objective individually on a scale of 1 to 10, with 10 being assigned to those objectives that are most desired, necessary, or urgent. The same rating number can be assigned to different objectives, and not all numbers will necessarily be used. Such a scale enables you to avoid wasting the efforts of yourself and your staff on objectives rated 1 and 2 when those same efforts could be much more fruitfully applied to objectives rated 9 or 10.

Two key overall objectives should be kept in mind at all times in establishing objectives and their supportive strategies: *return on capital* and *growth*. Improved return on capital is the essence of a turnaround. Inadequate growth leads to demise.

You now have a prioritized list of the places you want to go, with a quantified notation of any problems or opportunities you may encounter on the way to each place. You have also assigned a level of risk to each of these anticipated encounters.

Step 3. *How do we want to get there?* Strategic alternatives now enter the picture. Many companies utilize a high degree of sophistication in completing this step. Although they are not discussed here, you should be aware of the numerous outstanding techniques available that are designed to improve and maximize the selection of the best strategies from the alternatives. Some of these techniques utilize advanced mathematics with computer support. Others are manual and relatively simple to apply.

However, because this is your first try, and because turnarounds seldom need much more than sound basic management, a simple straightforward approach is again recommended.

Prepare a three-column work sheet for each agreed-on objective (see Figure 24). Note the pertinent objective at the top of each sheet.

Then, at a meeting with your immediate subordinates, develop alternative strategies for each objective.

This is best done by taking the objectives one at a time—starting with those rated 10, then those rated 9, and so on—and, through brainstorming, coming up with as many strategies as possible for attaining them. Complete the listing of alternative strategies for one objective before proceeding to the next.

In case you have more objectives than can be managed effectively, and because brainstorming is time- and energy-consuming, temporarily adjourn the session as often as you feel a rest is required. Don't be too concerned if you fail to cover all the objectives.

As soon as possible after the final adjournment you decided on, review those objectives, if any, that have not yet been strategized. Select from them the ones needed to construct a balanced plan. Say the Human Resources function has had little involvement in the objectives already strategized. Select a sufficient number of the remaining lower-priority objectives to provide a balanced involvement of Human Resources in the plan. Also se-

Figure 24. Strategic alternatives work sheet.

Strategic Alternatives Objective _____ _____ _____		Date _____ By _____
Alternative Strategies	Comments	Selection

lect from the remaining objectives the ones that consti-
tute a part of sound basic management but that may
not have been given a high priority. Protecting the assets of the enterprise might be one of these objectives.
Finally, pull out any objectives that have peculiar significance to you or your superiors; discard the remainder. Then, on your own, develop some alternative strategies for those lower-priority objectives that have been
selected.

Meet again with your staff to choose a strategy from
the alternatives offered for each alternative. Select the
alternative that you and your staff believe will best
achieve each stated objective and, in each case, check
off that alternative on your work sheet in the Selection

column. In the Comments column, be sure to indicate the reason for selection of that alternative strategy. Recheck all selected strategies for any cross-conflicts and resolve them.

Continue with the same procedure for the lower-priority objectives that you selected for inclusion in the plan. After a little massaging, your strategic plan will be complete.

Step 4. *Summarize the tentative strategic plan.* Put the plan together, beginning with the mission statement and followed by categorized objectives and strategies and sufficient documentation to support the major decisions therein. Include exhibits of projected sales, earnings statements, balance sheets, cash flow, and ROI.

Then decide whether or not to accept the plan as presented and to submit it for approval by higher authority, if such approval is required. In making this decision, three areas of judgment should be applied: (1) Is the plan consistent both in itself and within the overall framework of the organization? (2) Are the financial goals and requirements reasonable? (3) Can it be adequately managed by your organization? If so, move ahead. If not, restate the plan so that it will meet these three qualifications.

Step 5. *Implement and measure performance.* Convert strategies to measurable goals. Sometimes it's wise to list subordinate goals under each strategy before submitting the plan for board approval. This tends to reinforce the depth of thought given to the development and implementation of each stated strategy. However, as previously suggested, do not allow this step to delay plan approval.

These goals must be developed as early in the planning game as possible, because they transform the strategic plan into a vibrant entity. They may be in the form recommended for MWOs, with each planning goal then being converted to a personal objective. Each strategy should be supported by all the routine, problem-solving, innovative, and personal objectives necessary to assure its successful implementation.

Scheduling the Strategic Planning Process

It should now be evident that the strategic planning process involves a considerable amount of work. It should also be obvious that this work is not the type that lends itself to finite advanced scheduling, especially the first time around. Steps are best scheduled individually upon the completion of each prior step. It is imperative, though, to keep the planning program moving as rapidly as possible—while meeting the requirement of always managing it well.

To give some idea of how the process might be effectively scheduled, the following is typical for a medium-size company in which the staff has had some seminar training sessions.

Immediately following the training sessions, meet with the head of your Marketing function to agree on what is to be included in the analysis of your products, markets, and competition, and on when the marketing manager is to have the first draft completed. This step will probably take longer to complete than any of the others in the preplanning process.

Then meet with all the members of your staff; remind them of the accepted definitions of a mission statement and a strategy; request that they each list the current and recent objectives and strategies related to ther functional responsibility; and establish a meeting time for reviewing each list privately with each subordinate involved.

At this same staff meeting, a 1½-day staff meeting away from the plant should also be announced. This gathering should be scheduled to immediately follow submission of the preplanning lists. It will be held for the purposes of:

1. Establishing a tentative mission statement.
2. Firming up the list of all current and recent objectives and strategies.
3. Evaluating these objectives and strategies.
4. Evaluating external factors that are apt to have an impact on the business.
5. Testing existing objectives and strategies for cross-conflicts.

Prior to that follow-up meeting, arrange to have existing objectives and strategies categorized as recommended earlier.

Arrange for nearby daily and evening clerical support at the off-site sessions. This will be necessary to complete the tasks required to move from items one through five on the agenda.

After you have had sufficient time to work with the results of this session and with the product/market competitor analysis, a second, 2½-day off-site meeting should be scheduled. (Members of the staff should be encouraged to participate in whatever strategic planning activities are taking place between these two meetings. Such activities include follow-up work on the first meeting and preparation of a preliminary list of needed objectives.)

The purposes of the second meeting are to finalize the results of the first, to decide on the list of objectives that are to be achieved, to develop and evaluate alternative strategies for each objective, and to select the best strategies from these alternatives.

Again, nearby daily and evening clerical support may be needed.

After these sessions, you will be in a position to crystallize the strategic plan. At this point and possibly throughout the process, highlights should be reviewed with your immediate superior. Your usual personal business relationship should dictate the extent of such contact.

One final meeting is then required for the purpose

of reviewing the plan and deciding how and when the supporting goals are to be established and implemented. This meeting could take the form of a presentation rehearsal if the plan is to be submitted to higher authority for final approval.

Making the Strategic Plan Work

The strategies necessary to implement each objective have been selected; the strategies have been translated into individual goals; responsibility for attaining each goal has been assigned.

In many cases, those assigned that responsibility will have to develop task lists with further delegated responsibilities in order to attain their goals. Some lists may be extremely simple. However, a number of long-range objectives, such as product development, a new plant, a complicated financing program, or a change in human resource philosophies, will demand rather intricate logistics and scheduling to achieve. Without seeming to dictate "how" to the immediate subordinates responsible for each goal, you should take the time to assure yourself that adequate task lists are in place.

By definition, each goal must have an assigned means for measuring progress toward it. These means should be quickly collated into a reports package, which measures progress to goals and uncovers shortfalls in time for corrective action to be taken.

A word of caution in closing. The strategic plan is a highly sensitive document, one you certainly wouldn't want in the hands of a competitor. For that reason, its distribution should be stringently restricted.

14
Make It Work and Keep It Working

BY now, all the tools for the turnaround should be in place and functioning. Significant earnings progress should already have resulted from the short-range programs. Enthusiasm should be at a high level throughout the organization.

Two major challenges remain: to achieve first-year goals and to preserve the vitality of the planning programs over the long haul. How well both of these challenges are met depends primarily on your continuing commitment and involvement.

As long as you keep the pot on a lighted burner, the turnaround will continue to cook. The degree of heat applied must be adjusted from time to time in order to achieve a turnaround of gourmet quality. But the turnaround will surely collapse if it is left on the back burner for long.

Achieving First-Year Goals

Your turnaround program now includes eight planning tools that should be approximately, although not yet completely, in phase.

1. Long-range strategic plan.
2. Short-range plan.
3. MWO program.

4. Personnel staffing budget.
5. Income and expense budget.
6. Capital expenditures budget.
7. Cash flow budget.
8. Controls.

Obviously, these are all candidates for improvement, both individually and as an integrated package. Therefore, in addition to the first-year goals already established, it is well to include the objective of integrating all your planning programs. Fine-tuning of each element, and of the entire package, will take place almost automatically, as those involved gain more experience, reconfirm their commitment, and stay abreast of the state of the art of the techniques involved.

The best method for completely integrating all the programs is merely to go ahead and do it the next time around. Begin by quickly establishing and distributing an annual planning schedule. If your firm is on a fiscal year that coincides with the calendar year, a suggested schedule is:

Long-range strategic plan—June 15 of each year: Annually project a new fifth year, and modify the then-current plan to include known and readily accessible changes. In alternate years, reconstruct the plan from scratch, following each step outlined in Chapter 13, including creative brainstorming. In that most of the information will not change to any significant degree, this biennial revision will not demand nearly as much time as the initial effort did.

Short-range plan, including staffing, capital, and financial budgets—October 15 of each year: This should include an updated projection of the current year and a complete set of budgets for the following year. A new fifth year should be added to the capital budget. All of these documents should be congruent with the long-range strategic plans, or that plan should be amended by annotation to reflect any differences.

MWOs and quarterly budget updates—15th of the last

month of each quarter: These budget updates firm up the following quarter and add a new period, so that each update projects four quarters. MWOs and budgets are tied into the above-noted plans.

Control reports—regularly and continually: These reports should be improved, increased, or in some cases abandoned on an ongoing basis to best measure and ensure performance to plan.

Regular reminders may be required to prevent daily emergencies and attractive new projects from detouring the turnaround/growth program. Don't relax your tolerance level in accepting excuses for poor or late performance. Continue to insist that you be advised of any unresolved daily emergencies within 24 hours.

Don't delay in implementing your contingency plan, should external factors, such as a recessive economy, reach the level of impact that you originally targeted as requiring contingent action.

Like most good programs, your turnaround merits public relations support. All of your people are a part of the program and deserve to know how the plan is progressing. Most of them will want to know. To keep them involved and enthusiastic, inform them whenever a record of any sort is broken. This can be done by posting notices, by holding group meetings with employees, and by always having at hand a relevant remark to be made in passing.

Be on the lookout for landmark performances in all areas. For example, monthly sales records may be good news to most employees but may only mean more headaches and a heavier workload for those in accounts receivable. On the other hand, an announcement of a record for collections, or for fewest days of receivables outstanding, will be a positive energizer for the accounts receivable staff.

The president of one company with which I am familiar requires each functional manager to maintain a notebook of departmental records and to notify him immediately whenever one is broken. He credits much of his company's success to his ability to "always be prepared to congratulate."

A Plan For Financial Incentives

Financial incentives may also be used effectively in conjunction with a turnaround program. The purpose of an incentive plan is to further the achievement of earnings growth, at an acceptable rate of return on investment, by rewarding employees for their contribution to that accomplishment.

But in order to work, incentives must be established with extreme care. Some types of managerial bonus plans work very well; the majority, however, have missed their targets. Plans that have failed to achieve their intended results have failed for a number of reasons, of which some of the most prevalent are:

1. They are too complex for the participants to understand. A regular bonus check, which the recipient does not really comprehend, may promote the attitude that the company is a good place to work, but it will do little more. In fact, should the amount of these checks decline, a negative reaction might follow.

2. They pay too little or too much. A bonus in the pittance neighborhood will have little direct effect on your objective. Extremely high bonuses are best applied on an individual basis for achievements that can be measured accurately.

3. They are established on a bad base. Some are designed to encourage short-range performance to the degree that they encourage long-range strangulation. Needed capital investments are postponed, year after year, because going through with them will have a negative effect on the current year's bonus.

Some bonus plans are directly related to attainment of MWO objectives and encourage goal setting that is far too conservative. Compensation must have a direct relationship to individual achievement. But when rewards are tied completely to attainment of individual objectives, there are far too many people who will aim for lower targets or complain that others have easier ones to achieve.

Other plans are based on erroneous anticipations or bad assumptions and are abandoned when the errors are realized. Typical of this group are plans with no ceilings—plans that, when established, did have an assumed ceiling of, "We'll never be able to do better than that." One company, believing it could reduce its labor costs by as much as 15 percent, hired several new supervisors and offered them a ceilingless bonus plan aimed at that goal. When labor costs dropped by 35 percent, the new supervisors were earning more than most senior managers.

My experiences favor one type of plan that works well when properly administered. It is simple and easy to understand and maintain. Twice a year, participating employees are paid a bonus directly related to the pretax earnings of the company for the preceding six months. A bonus application factor is decided on and applied to the company profit percentage. The resulting percentage is then applied to each participating employee's earnings for the last six months to arrive at the bonus amount. For example, a firm realizes a 15 percent pretax profit for the six-month period being used and the application factor is 70 percent (about the right level). All participating employees receive a lump sum bonus of 15 percent × 70 percent, or 10.5 percent, of what their total straight-time pay had been during that six months.

Such a plan is usually effective in a turnaround situation. To install it, a base earnings target must first be adopted. If the company had been losing money, a base of zero is recommended. Participating employees would thus share in all profits. If the company had been in the black before the turnaround program was initiated, a profit percentage slightly higher than the past two years' average is suggested as a base. For example, if the concern had averaged 4.2 percent pretax profits over the past two years, a base of 5 or 6 percent might be chosen.

Figure 25. Turnaround program checklist.

| Item | Action Dates | | Comments | |
	Last Done	Next Scheduled	On Last Action	For Next Action
1. Review programs with key staff members.				
2. Review programs with all employees.				
3. Audit each business function.				
4. Review performance of each key employee.				
5. Maintain sound working relationships with key outside contacts.				
6. Solicit opportunities from key personnel.				
7. Maintain an integrated MWO program.				
8. Update budgets.				
9. Update strategic long-range plan.				

In such a case, participants would receive no bonus for any six-month period in which pretax earnings did not exceed the 5 or 6 percent base. But they would receive 70 percent of the total profit percentage for all six-month periods in which earnings were above the established base.

The decision of who should participate depends on a number of factors, not the least of which are cost considerations and whether or not a union is involved.

One suggested approach is to adopt a standard application factor in the area of 70 percent, and to apply it to all employees included in the MWO program. This gives higher-level managers a head start, encourages expansion downward of the MWO program, as well as participation in it, and provides for a sufficient degree of participation to achieve the intended objective.

Keep the Program Working

The techniques required to keep a turnaround program working effectively are those already discussed throughout this book, with one critical addition—continuing education.

A working checklist of the included techniques is provided for the turnaround manager as Figure 25 of this chapter. It should be kept near at hand, annotated with new thoughts as they occur, and reviewed and filled out each quarter.

My closing comment on the importance of continuing education is this: Don't merely encourage it. Force it. Continued learning keeps minds active and growing. Active and growing minds keep companies active and growing. Insist that your key subordinates attend seminars, trade shows, and the like, on a regular, repetitive basis. Keep them creative and at least parallel with the latest developments in all fields affecting the progress of your company. It's the best investment you can make.

Index